Glimpses of Gwent

Book 2

Dr Gareth D John

DEDICATION

*Make no more pretences
Of new discoveries, whilst yet thine own
And nearest, little world is still unknown.*

George Herbert
'Travels At Home' (1633)

Old Bakehouse Publications

Abertillery

ISBN 1 874538 34 4

Published in the U.K. by
Old Bakehouse Publications
Church Street,
Abertillery, Gwent NP13 1EA
Telephone: 01495 212600 Fax: 01495 216222
www.mediamaster.co.uk/oldbakebooks

Made and printed in the UK
by J.R. Davies (Printers) Ltd.

WILLIAM JEFFERSON CLINTON

Dr Gareth D John
c/o Old Bakehouse Publications
Church Street
Abertillery
Gwent
Wales
NP13 1EA
UNITED KINGDOM

Dear Gareth,

Thank you very much for your interesting and informative book, *'Glimpses of Gwent'*. I greatly appreciate your thoughtfulness in offering me a copy.

My recent visit to South Wales was wonderful, and I am pleased to have your book as a reminder.

All the very best to you.

Sincerely,

Bill Clinton

Bill Clinton
June 2001

President
United States of America
(1992-2000)

CONTENTS

MAP OF CONTENTS

INTRODUCTION

CONCLUSION

ACKNOWLEDGEMENTS

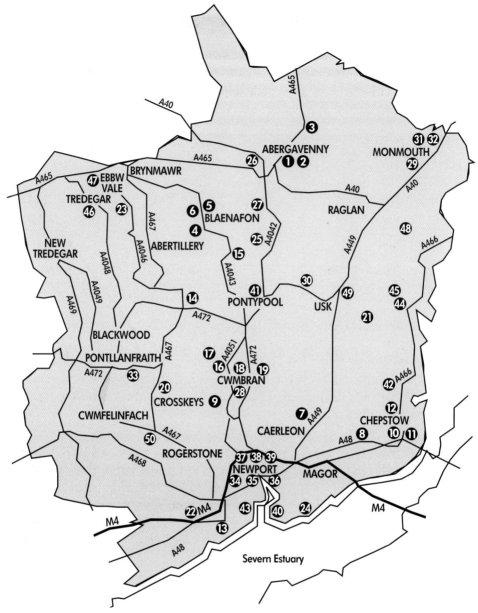

Introduction

Following the encouraging success of *'Glimpses of Gwent'* (1999), I have been inundated with requests to write a sequel and, after due consideration, I have decided to do so.

Hopefully, this second collection of narratives will prove just as popular and as informative as the first compilation. Again, the 'mix' comprises both 'old and new'; certain themes may be familiar, but much of the text describes places that remain outside the mainstream of everyday life. Relevant photographs enhance the subject matter. The listing is neither definitive nor exhaustive - merely another personal selection.

The map on the preceding page targets locations mentioned in the text and should prove a valuable guide to those unfamiliar with the topography of the County.

The traditional 'heavy' industries of coal, iron and steelmaking, which for centuries dominated and sustained the growth of the region, are all but extinct: the ravaged landscape has been restored to something resembling its former self, following sympathetic reclamation programmes. Modern, lighter and more environmentally-friendly industries now contribute to the economic and social prosperity of the County.

It is heartening and indeed fitting that the ancient remains of the ironworks at Blaenafon and the surrounding area, for so long in the vanguard of the Industrial Revolution, should gain the prestigious accolade of World Heritage Status during the year 2000. By contrast, the cluster of ruined, small-scale, water-powered ironworks nestling along the Angidy Valley, Tintern, and which predates Blaenafon by well over a century, continues to receive scant attention by historians, industrial archaeologists and tourists alike.

Recently, many of the place names in Gwent have reverted to their proper Welsh spellings - most noticeably in the heavily anglicised County Borough of Monmouthshire.

Finally, I hope this book gives much pleasure to the reader; also, that it whets the appetite of curiosity to explore what is, after all, a mystical and enchanted land, a border county steeped in legend and romance, and with an unique history and identity rooted in the Welsh language and culture. Iechyd Da!

G.D.J.
September 2001

A Brush With The Past

Visitors to Abergavenny are in for a real treat. For at High Cross shopping centre, and impossible to miss, is an eye-catching, gigantic outdoor mural.

The mural, painted by the highly talented and enterprising local artist Frances Baines, was commissioned by Abergavenny Town Council with the full support of Monmouthshire County Borough Council. Its purpose? Not merely to commemorate the new millennium, but rather to depict the fascinating and turbulent history of this ancient border town. The mural took 7 weeks to paint; it was officially unveiled during July 2000.

The mural is a skilful composite of the changing life of the town, its beleaguered Norman castle, and the surrounding countryside over the past thousand years. The artist's source material, carefully researched, comprised old photographs, wood cuts and the impressions of celebrated antiquaries.

Two large central panels display the town as it was in 1100 and 1665 A.D. Other periods portrayed are mid Victorian and, relatively recently, the mid 1930s. The skyline of the backdrop is dominated by the instantly recognisable Skirrid Fawr - the mystical Holy Mountain with its jagged cleft and legendary association with the Crucifixion of Christ.

Incidentally, Frances Baines is no stranger to the art of murals. Far from it. Her first work was completed some 20 years ago. Other distinctive murals followed, but it was not until 1997 that she finally decided to establish her own business, Greenfield Murals. Since then success has followed upon success. Nowadays, her artistry is greatly admired and much in demand; also, she has regularly collaborated with youngsters on projects throughout Gwent schools.

The 'Abergavenny Mural', as it has become known, is a strikingly colourful and imaginative work of art, a rich 'woven' tapestry befitting Abergavenny. It continues to provoke interest and discussion from passers-by, and is certain to captivate all who marvel at its full splendour. Yes, a veritable treasure, a wholly delightful 'brush' with the past.

A Dastardly Deed!

Abergavenny Castle is often dismissed by tourists as hardly worth a visit. A pity, really, for while little survives of this once-mighty Norman stronghold its beleaguered and blood-stained walls witnessed an act of despicable treachery, an atrocity without parallel in the annals of conflict between the Welsh and their Norman overlords.

In 1172 the castle was captured by Sitsyllt ap Dyfnwal (ancestor of the famous Cecil family). Over the following years life generally became less turbulent, with Welsh and Normans co-existing uneasily but peaceably. Then in 1175, on the advice of his influential brother-in-law, Rhys ap Gruffydd (the Lord Rhys was a staunch ally of Henry II), Sitsyllt relinquished the castle to the Norman Lordship. This act of amity was subsequently to prove a grave error of judgement.

Delighted with this unexpected gesture of goodwill, King Henry reciprocated by inviting Sitsyllt and his fellow Welshmen to his court at Gloucester. Indignation was set aside and Sitsyllt was granted the King's pardon; past violent crimes were forgiven and bonds of trust and friendship forged. The Welsh returned home well-satisfied; things augured well for the future.

However, shortly afterwards William de Braose succeeded to the Lordship of Abergavenny and became the castle's most notorious incumbent. Mindful that his uncle, Henry Fitz-Milo, had been brutally murdered by the Welsh, William conceived a wicked plan to rid himself of his troublesome Welsh neighbours once and for all. Under the guise of celebrating the reconciliation and the cessation of hostilities, he extended a hearty invitation to Sitsyllt and the principal Welsh chieftains to attend a sumptuous banquet at the castle. Thus, on Christmas Day 1175, the unsuspecting Welshmen gathered before the castle gates bent on taking advantage of Norman hospitality, completely unaware of the fate that was about to befall them. Yes, William de Braose it seemed was the genial host.

True to the custom of the day the Welsh laid down their weapons before entering the Great Hall to partake of good food and strong drink. And enjoy themselves they certainly did. But at the height of the feasting and merriment, and after countless toasts to everlasting friendship, William unexpectedly rose to his feet and made a royal ordinance that henceforth all Welsh chieftains should take an oath 'that no traveller by the waie amongst them should beare any bow or other weapon'. The Welsh objected vehemently; their proud, independent nature would never allow them to agree to such an unreasonable demand.

William's mood changed abruptly. At a pre-arranged signal the great doors were closed and bolted, and his men-at-arms set upon the hapless guests. Unable to defend themselves all were ruthlessly butchered - except one. Prince Iorwerth of Caerleon escaped the bloodshed by procuring a Norman's sword and using the darkness of the night. During the slaughter de Braose piously intoned 'Let this be done in the Lord's name'.

By perpetrating such a heinous crime William de Braose had violated one of the most ancient and sacred traditions of Welsh culture - the duty of hospitality, thereby establishing himself in Welsh history as the greatest blackguard of that age of barbarism, the 'Ogre of Abergavenny'. The sense of outrage felt amongst the Welsh nation was immense. Seven years after the cowardly slaughter Iorwerth

of Caerleon stormed Abergavenny Castle to ensure 'the completeness of the cruelty'. This was the Welsh way.

Like all the worst villains de Braose's luck eventually ran out. Thirty years later, in 1209, he and his grasping wife, Maud, alienated King John who confiscated his estates and titles. William fled to France to die a wretch and a pauper. Maud and their eldest son were imprisoned in Windsor Castle and left to starve to death.

Abergavenny Castle was all but demolished in 1404 when Owain Glyndŵr besieged and ransacked the town. Further ravages in 1645 by Charles I reduced it to its present sorry state; the gatehouse with its broken archway, the masonry of the two towers, and the connecting outer walls, together with the foundations of the Norman keep are all that remain.

The ghosts of those massacred on that fateful day in 1175 still haunt the site of the ruined Great Hall. For the sheer violence of the dastardly deed is a reminder that the clout of the mace was the ultimate sanction in such unruly times. And who, nowadays, strolling around the castle's picturesque grounds could ever imagine the terrible secret its crumbling fragments conceal.

Incidentally, the name de Braose (or de Breos) lives on - as pedigree cattle. How appropriate!

The Holy Mountain

Holy mountains. What uplifting things! But do they really exist? Certainly. For in the minds of countless generations eager to explain natural phenomena, these awe-inspiring mountaintops have long been regarded as the handiwork of the Almighty. And the Skirrid Fawr on the outskirts of Abergavenny - its Welsh name is Ysgyryd Fawr, meaning 'holy place' - is no exception.

Various tales are told about the Skirrid. The most widely held belief is that the massive cleft at its northern end - its most striking feature - occurred when 'the earth did quake and the rocks rent by lightning' during the darkness of Christ's Crucifixion. A much older legend, more fanciful perhaps, is that during the Great Flood the tip of the mountain was accidentally knocked off as Noah's Ark sailed over it!

Other stories maintain that the hollow near the summit which marks the site of an ancient Roman Catholic chapel is really the heel-print of Jack O'Kent. This was formed when the giant leapt the 4 miles from the summit of the nearby Sugar Loaf. Egged on by the sneering and contemptuous remarks of the Devil at such a meagre feat, Jack thereupon picked up three enormous boulders and flung them eastward over 12 miles to Trellech, where they remain to this very day.

During the religious persecutions of the 17th-century, devout Catholics regularly made the steep and arduous ascent in large numbers to the summit, there to gather unhindered for Mass in the chapel of St. Michael. In later times, open-air anniversary services were conducted on the mountaintop upon Michaelmas Eve. Nowadays,

all that remains of the tiny chapel are two upright stones about 2 feet high with chamfered edges where the entrance once stood; also, scanty traces of its foundations. So convinced of the mountaintop's mystical powers were the country-folk within the parish of Llanfihangel that until very recent times it was a common practice to remove a small quantity of consecrated soil from the chapel area to sprinkle over the coffins of the dead during burial. (Has the traditional burial changed that much down the ages?) Farmers, too, gathered the sacred soil to scatter upon the floors of cattle sheds to ward off disease and pestilence, and to strew upon their farmland to bring good fortune and bounteous harvests.

When the celebrated antiquary, Archdeacon Coxe, toured the County in 1801 he ventured to the summit on foot. Though exhausted upon reaching the narrow rugged precipice, he marvelled at 'the boundless expanse around and beneath'. Overcome with a sense of wonder, the great man claimed that he could see 'the spires of Hereford Cathedral gleam in the distant prospect'.

From the summit the views are indeed spectacular; some 1600 feet directly below stretches the lush pastoral of the fertile Usk Valley; the nearby distinctive features of the Blorenge and Sugar Loaf and, much further afield, the menacing dark outlines of the Black Mountains of Central Wales.

And what could be more delightful in springtime than to marvel at the lower slopes of this miniature Alpine peak thickly covered with bluebells; its farms and white-washed cottages snugly sheltering beneath the brooding summit; and in autumn and winter its upper reaches clad in a mass of purple heather and bracken. For here, surely, is one of the Master's finest works!

The Dog Stone

Ramblers wandering across the windswept crown of Coity Mountain, overlooking Blaenafon, (and many do!) are usually surprised to find a prominent memorial to a favoured canine friend. For at this bleak and isolated spot lies the buried remains of a dog renowned for its prowess as a hunter.

The animal's grave is marked by an 8 feet high cast-iron headstone, popularly known as the 'Dog Stone', bearing the following inscription:

IN
MEMORY OF
CARLO
A CELEBRATED
SETTER
THE PROPERTY
OF
H. M. KENNARD ESQ.
CRUMLIN HALL
ACCIDENTALLY
SHOT
AUGUST 12TH
1864

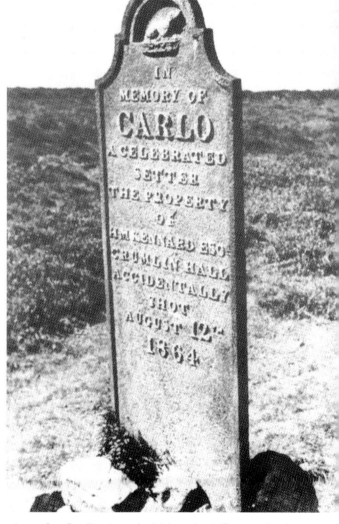

It is difficult to imagine how a large dog could meet this kind of fate on such open terrain. Yet it must be remembered that, traditionally, dogs were kept not merely as household pets, but as 'working dogs'. Therefore, they were expected to 'earn' their keep. And the grouse moors hereabouts were formerly managed by game-keepers employed by the local iron-masters for the pleasure of hunting and shooting. Even today there is game in abundance - especially the much-prized Red Grouse. For the patchwork of grass, newly seeded heather (for feeding) and old heather (for nesting), have long combined to create an ideal habitat for Grouse.

Clearly, Carlo the Red Setter was a faithful servant to his master, H.M. Kennard, general manager of Blaenafon Ironworks (and a member of the family that designed and constructed Crumlin Viaduct). Yes, a remarkable dog.

Blaenafon Ironworks

At the top of the Afon Llywd Valley stands the ancient remains of Blaenafon Ironworks. This famous ironworks of Thomas Hill and Samuel Hopkins was a milestone in the history of the Industrial Revolution.

For at this site in 1788-89 the very first purpose-built, multi-furnace ironworks in Wales was constructed. Utilising the most up-to-date technology, a bank of coke-burning blast furnaces was set into the hillside enabling easy filling from the upper level. Each furnace was superheated with air blown in by a steam engine, thereby smelting iron ore into 'pig iron'.

But why was such a remote and inhospitable place as Blaenafon chosen for this industrial 'adventure'? Simply because the surrounding hills held an abundance of the resources necessary for iron production - iron ore, coal for coking, and limestone for removing earthen impurities.

The booming development at Blaenafon attracted those eager or desperate for employment. Two rare survivors of the housing stock built for these immigrant iron-workers between 1789 and 1792 are 'Stack Square' and 'Engine Row', terraced houses accommodating families of up to eight - plus lodgers! (Other ruined dwellings adjacent to the ironworks were unceremoniously demolished during the 1960s and 1970s).

By 1796 Blaenafon was the second largest ironworks in Wales, annually producing some 5,400 tons of iron. But at considerable human cost. The working conditions were appalling; all able-bodied members of the household toiled long hours to earn a mere pittance. 'Fine strong girls' daily smashed ironstone with sledgehammers, while boys as young as 7 years of age carted it off to feed the ever-hungry furnaces.

Until 1856 the making of steel was beset by technical problems, such as how to get rid of impurities like phosphorous? The Bessemer process began to change things. And at Blaenafon in 1878 Sidney Gilchrist Thomas and his cousin Percy Carlyle Gilchrist successfully experimented in making fine steel cheaply and on a large scale from the local phosphorous - containing ore: the wealthy American, Andrew Carnegie, purchased the formula. Paradoxically, this invention made the world richer, but Blaenafon the poorer as the growth in steelmaking elsewhere far outstripped that of Britain.

Blaenafon Ironworks operated for well over a century before becoming obsolete: the last furnace was extinguished in 1904. The works lay neglected and ignored for many years. Fortunately, though, its industrial importance was recognised; it is now in the care of the Welsh Historic Monuments Agency, CADW.

Recent years have seen an ongoing conservation programme of the existing works; much of the site is currently accessible to the public. The remaining furnaces, casting houses, truck shop, etc., still paint a vivid picture of iron-production and the workers' lifestyles.

Most impressive and dominating the site is the massive water balance tower. Built in 1839 to ease the moving of goods from one level to another, it ingeniously used water as a counterweight to the cargo. Simple but effective.

Without doubt, Blaenafon Ironworks is the best surviving example of a late 18th-century ironworks in Western Europe. And the nearby housing stock is proof of the grim reality of early industrial life, of a community struggling to survive amidst hardship and a bleak and barren moorland landscape. Thankfully, such times are in the past.

On 30th November, 2000, the town of Blaenafon was granted World Heritage Status in recognition as the birthplace of the Industrial Revolution which changed the face of the modern world. Yes, the small town can justifiably feel proud of its ranking alongside such attractions as the Great Wall of China, the Pyramids of Egypt, the Taj Mahal of India and Stonehenge.

The award of such a prestigious accolade will surely revive the town's ailing economy by a massive influx of foreign tourists, witness a resurgence of inward investment, and generally boost Blaenafon's image as a centre of universal interest and importance. Well, whoever would have thought it possible? Unbelievable.

Full Steam Ahead

Steam railways belong to a bygone era. Or do they? For throughout Britain there are many privately owned railways with preserved steam locomotives and accompanying rolling stock. The Pontypool & Blaenafon Railway based at Furnace Sidings, Blaenafon, is very much an evocative reminder of the 'golden age of steam'. The railway is operated solely by volunteers, all members of the Pontypool & Blaenafon Railway Company (1983) Limited.

Originally, the railway extended from Pontypool to Brynmawr with the northern section operated by the London & North Western Railway (later the LMS) down as far as Abersychan and Talywain where it connected with the Great Western Railway to Pontypool, and thence by other lines to the coastal port of Newport.

As a wartime economy measure the line was closed to passengers in May 1941, but never reinstated. Even so, the section between Blaenafon and Pontypool continued to carry heavy mineral traffic from Big Pit and other local collieries until 1980 when the track was lifted.

Nowadays, only a minor part of the northern section remains. This runs from the main station at Furnace Sidings, through a landscape stunning in its stark ruggedness, to the terminus at Whistle Halt beside the aptly named Whistle Inn at Garn-yr-Erw. Whistle Halt stands at over 1,300 feet above sea level and is the highest (and probably the most windswept!) station in the land. Incidentally, the Whistle Inn is renowned for its unique collection of miners' lamps, sad relics of the once proud and mighty coal-mining industry of Gwent.

The railway boasts an impressive array of steam engines, both in working order and at static exhibition. These include 'Nora', an 0-4-0 Saddle Tank which formerly worked the Blaenafon collieries system; 'Austerity', an 0-6-0 Saddle Tank from Mountain Ash; a GWR 0-6-0 Pannier Tank which fronted the Marriott Hotel in central Cardiff for several years before arriving at Blaenafon.

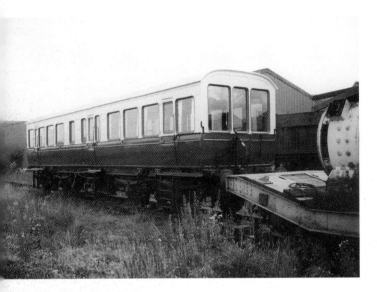

In 1987 five GWR Swindon locomotives were rescued from that most famous 'graveyard of steam' - Barry Scrapyard. Of particular worth is 'Bickmarsh Hall', a 4-6-0, which hauled express trains throughout the GWR region. The others worked the South Wales Valleys on 'coal duty'.

The railway also possesses several diesels, ranging from main-line locomotives to tiny industrial 0-4-0s.

Several former BR Mark 1 carriages provide the backbone of the passenger carrying capacity. Other more unusual ex-GWR and ex-LSWR carriages await restoration. Undoubtedly, though, the star of the show is the magnificent Manchester & Milford Railway saloon of 1892 which has been lovingly restored to its former glory.

Lastly, but not least, is the assortment of mixed freight; a crane wagon, bitumen tanks, 'china clays', coal trucks, brake vans, amongst others, complete the line up.

Apart from public holidays, the Pontypool & Blaenafon Railway provides a regular service each weekend during the summer months, offering the inquisitive visitor an unique opportunity to step back in time and relive the bygone days of 'steam'. Annual events include Easter Bunny Specials, Lucky Dip Specials and Santa Specials - all favourites with the children.

And what of the future? Plans are already well advanced for the railway to extend its current operation down the Afon Llwyd Valley; also, northward to Waunafon. A major tourist attraction in the making? Hopefully so.

Isca Morrismen

A suitable case for treatment! Yes, that is often the reaction of those unfamiliar with the ancient tradition of Morris Dancing. After all, grown men cavorting around to the jingle of bells while brandishing thick wooden sticks, waving white handkerchiefs and quaffing tankards of foaming ale! Well! Despite this seemingly bizarre pastime there is a far more serious side to the Morris.

Deeply rooted in prehistory, Morris Dancing is the oldest known form of dancing and was the first to actually have been written down. Whilst its origins remain somewhat obscure, it was probably part of a primitive pagan ritual-ceremonial intended to bring good luck and fertility to the home and to the land.

Isca Morrismen delight in perpetuating this distinctive and important part of folklore. Founded in 1976 by three experienced dancers eager to revive an almost forgotten tradition in Gwent, the group takes its name from the Roman Fortress which once stood at Caerleon upon-Usk.

Isca's 'kit' reflects both the traditional Morris costume and the national colours of Wales - red, white and green - with a smart red sash upon which is mounted a Roman helmet badge. The Monmouth Caps worn were formerly knitted locally and were one of the earliest surviving medieval knitted garments. The white shirt, green corduroy trousers, the baldrics, the bell pads on the legs and the compulsory pure white handkerchiefs complete a most impressive outfit.

The dances are primarily from the Welsh Borders, the Cotswolds and from Lichfield, areas long-steeped in the Morris tradition. Yet like all 'living' traditions, Isca's

repertoire is continually evolving with new dances reflecting aspects of modern society.

The dances are virile, wild even, and skilfully performed by a team of six or eight men. The 'processional on' and 'processional off' dances in the repertoire are vestiges of the old tradition. However, most of the dances are performed as 'set' dances on the spot with two lines of three men facing each other. Central to each dance is some theme of challenge such as hand-clapping, stick clashing, stamping and shouting - or merely leaping about. All harmless fun, really!

The dance steps may appear haphazard but they actually conform to precise sequences or 'figures'. Likewise, the music is an equally important element and must at all times fit each dance: this is especially true in the jumps or 'capers' where the music slows down to approximately half the main dance steps. Yet as the pulsating and repetitive sixteen-bar music demonstrates, order and symmetry of form are paramount. In bygone times virtually every village had its own Morris dancers ably accompanied by a fiddler. Sadly, by the close of the 19th-century the sides had dwindled to a mere few.

In Wales, Morris Dancing ended as a folk art with the rise of the nonconformist church who likened such activities to the work of the Devil. This great wave of religious fervour 'swept everything before it at the full-tide, bore on its crest the form of hatred of high musical art and instruments'. The latter quote refers specifically to the fiddle as an accompaniment to any form of dancing - and in particular for the local Morris side.

Nowadays, the fiddle has largely been superseded by the stronger and more strident melodeon. But not altogether.

Isca's touring season begins with the annual display in the Amphitheatre at Caerleon at 5.15 a.m (yes, the time is correct!) on the 1st May. Thereafter, the Morrismen perform regularly at welcoming hostelries throughout the length and breadth of Gwent... 'bringing entertainment to the community and providing the men themselves with the opportunity to enjoy good ale!' How very true. Happily, the tradition of ritual-ceremonial dancing is still alive, for Isca Morris is indeed living history.

The Forgotten City

Caerwent is a peaceful, sleepy village set in gently undulating countryside. Yet during the Roman occupation of Britain, Caerwent was the most important centre west of the River Severn. For here stood Venta Silurum. Founded late in the 1st-century, in about 75 A.D., Caerwent became the civil township of the Romans while they were building the legionary fortress of Isca at nearby Caerleon-upon-Usk.

And what a bustling centre of trade and commerce the walled town must have been. Four gates gave entry to the town, with parallel and right-angle streets dividing the town into blocks of 'insulae'. All the expected civic amenities were present - a forum (market place), a basilica (town hall), temples, public baths, villas, shops, wine shops and taverns. How little times have changed! The basilica had richly painted walls and decorative mosaic floors. The public baths were heated by an intricate network of hypocausts. Nobles and merchants prospered and built fine spacious villas - while their Silurian slaves stoked the furnaces which kept a continuous stream of hot air flowing through the underfloor hypocausts - an early form of central heating!

There is evidence to suggest that a Christian community existed throughout the Roman presence; a pewter dish excavated bears the unmistakable ancient Christian symbol - the Chi-Rho.

Caerwent remained occupied until well into the 4th-century. But with the gradual disintegration of the Roman civic system the town fell into steady decline and was eventually abandoned. What happened following the withdrawal of the Romans

from Britain to defend their homeland against the menacing Barbarians is obscure, though a Romano-British way of life probably persisted: the silence of the Dark Ages shrouds much fascinating history, mostly untold.

Caerwent is mentioned in the Domesday Book as Caruen or Carven. The Normans certainly settled here and built a small castle. Only a grassy mound at the south-east corner of the town wall remains.

In the 16th-century the antiquary, John Leland, wrote of Caerwent: 'It was some time a faire and large cyte. The places where the iii gates was yet appeare and the most parte of the waulle yet standith but all to minischyde and torne.'

Nowadays, the most impressive feature about Caerwent is its massive Roman walls which, remarkably, have survived the passage of time largely intact. The wall is traceable virtually all

around the former town; the northern gateway still stands beside the village inn of that name.

The town wall originally stood about 20 feet high and remains 11 feet wide at its base and 8 feet at the top. A rectangular area of some 44 acres is enclosed surrounded by an earthen bank and ditch. Early in the 4th-century towers were built into the perimeter wall to strengthen the defences, suggesting a period of unrest. The present road through the village is the old Roman road from London to Caerleon which passed through the original east and west gates of the Roman settlement.

The lower stone courses of shops and villas, and other civilian buildings can still be viewed. The ruins of the once mighty Roman Temple lie a mere 50 yards east of the parish church of St. Stephen.

Systematic excavations during the past century have revealed much about everyday life in the old town. Many antiquities are displayed in the museum at Newport, such as coins, fragments of pottery, glazed tiles, fine examples of wall-painting, portions of brightly patterned mosaic floor, etc.

By contrast, two sizeable stones stand in the porch of St. Stephen's Church. The larger stone, unearthed on the village green, bears an inscription to Tiberius Claudius Paulinus, Commander of the Second Augustan Legion at Caerleon. The smaller stone, found in 1924, formed the pedestal of a statue erected in 152 A.D. dedicated to the heathen god, Mars-Ocelus. The Romans were clearly prepared to assimilate the Celtic deity Ocelus, also a warrior god, with their own god.

During the early 20th-century numerous skeletons were discovered just outside the walls of the town, showing that the Romans respected the dead and gave proper burial rites in an organised cemetery; no burials were permitted inside a Roman town.

Caerwent is an unique example of a civilian settlement in Wales and certainly one of the most impressive sites in the whole of Roman Britain. And what archaeological treasures lie hidden beneath the modern houses and their gardens? No doubt a great many. Yes, the 'Camp of the Went' holds much of interest and is well worth a visit!

In God's Acre

Castell-y-Bŵch. What a name to conjure with! Rolling off a fluent Welshman's lips it is sheer poetry. But what does it mean? Bŵch in Welsh means buck (as in that of a male animal); yet in folklore it is also associated with a giant, Bŵch Gawr (Bŵch the Giant), who long ago lived at Castell-y-Bŵch. Very little is known about him, though apparently he fathered six sons each of whom became as huge as their father. What a veritable amazon his wife must have been! Poor Bŵch ended his days by having his head cut off. His sons had their 'castles' throughout the County and over the border in Glamorgan.

Castell-y-Bŵch is an isolated hamlet on a ridge aptly named Cefn Vynoche, that is, the monks' ridge. It overlooks the lush pastoral of Henllys Vale with its undulating fields and copses; and beyond, in the far distance the shining, silver-ribboned Severn Sea; the great range of Mynydd Maen acts as a backcloth, rising up steeply, silhouetted starkly against the expansive skyline. The heart of the hamlet revolves around the ancient inn of the same name. Though extensively modernised in recent years, it still retains some of its original character, such as stout oak beams and flag-stone floors - and good ale.

In the distant past, monks journeying from Llantarnam Abbey along the ancient trackway en route to the mysterious and mystical tumulus, Twm Barlwm on the crown of the southern end of Mynydd Maen, surely paused at the inn to rest their weary legs and seek refreshment with a pint or two of traditional ale or cider. And, presumably, on the return journey too!

Close by is Zoar Chapel, a simple stone building opened in 1836 to serve the spiritual needs of the rural community. Now it stands empty, abandoned by those it

had served so faithfully for over a century-and-a-half. A pity, really. For the burial ground contains many fine and interesting tombstones which, mellowed by age and clad with ivy, mirror the lives of those who worked the land hereabouts. Dotting either side of the ridge are picturesque stone cottages (mostly modernised) and white-washed farmhouses.

And did that famous son of Newport, the tramp-poet W.H. Davies, stroll idly in quietude along the shy and winding leafy lane from Llantarnam, past the grand old manor-house of Pentre Bach, and make the steep ascent to the top of the ridge, there to slake his thirst at the Castell-y-Bŵch inn with a glass of ale, 'mild and yet satisfying, frothy and yet without gas'? And then to watch the sun sink slowly over the softening contours of the purple mountain ranges? Most probably.

Castell-y-Bŵch remains largely unspoilt by the passage of centuries, a world of loveliness beyond the edge of time. And it is to be hoped that the menacing tentacles of residential development of expanding Cwmbran will not encroach and obliterate forever this most ancient of settlements in the same way it has to nearby Henllys village centre. Time alone will tell.

Family Matters

The church of St. Mary's, Chepstow, contains a number of highly interesting and unusual memorials. Not the least of these is an imposing 17th-century tomb that no visitor can possibly fail to notice due to its garish yet attractive quaintness - that of the irrepressible Margaret Cleyton.

Margaret was the wealthy daughter of John Maddock of Wollastone, Gent. She married Thomas Shipman and bore him **twelve** children. A veritable dynasty! Thomas died in 1591. 'Margaret the Relict' later remarried, to Richard Cleyton; he died in 1605.

The communal tomb dated 1620 is a splendid edifice in stone. Beneath its canopy are the effigies of her two husbands, one pale and the other

rosy-cheeked, and identically dressed in doublet and hose, kneeling in an attitude of prayer above her recumbent form; she lies in a red robe and white ruff. On the panel below, kneeling before a lectern as 'weepers', are her two sons and ten daughters by her first husband. The two eldest girls are wearing high 'Dame' hats indicating they had already married; the others are huddled together.

Recently, this unique Jacobean tomb has been repainted by local artist Keith Underwood in what is thought to resemble its original interactive colours with black and red predominating.

Margaret's town house still stands next to the town archway; today it serves as a Citizens Advice Bureau and Tourist Information Centre.

Without doubt, Margaret enjoyed an active and fruitful life. The Cleyton tomb is a memorial befitting a most colourful and remarkable lady.

The Regicide

The Norman Castle at Chepstow, the oldest castle in Britain, stands proudly rooted to the limestone cliffs high above the swirling waters of the River Wye. Its most eventful and stirring period was during the Civil War when it was garrisoned for Charles I; it eventually succumbed to the onslaughts of Cromwell and his troops. Yet, the most singular and intriguing episode in its long, chequered history was the 'stay' of the regicide Henry Marten.

Marten was a staunch Puritan and extreme anti-Royalist, one of the most zealous of Cromwell's supporters. A Member of Parliament during Charles I's reign, he was well known for his outspoken and inflammatory views. More significantly, he was one of the judges of the High Court of Justice responsible for deciding the fate of King Charles. It is reputed that after Cromwell had added his signature to the King's death warrant and accidentally splashed ink into Marten's face whilst passing the quill, Marten merely smiled and bespattered the Protector in similar fashion.

Following the Restoration of the monarchy in 1660 the Royalists gained their revenge by putting the principal signatories to Charles' death warrant on trial at the Old Bailey. Henry Marten was found guilty and condemned to death by hanging - only to be reprieved upon appeal to the House of Lords who commuted the sentence to life imprisonment.

After a brief spell in the Tower of London, Marten was brought to Chepstow Castle where he spent the next 20 years. He lived in Bigod's Tower, a large round tower in the south-east corner of the court to the left of the Great Gatehouse. Henceforth, the tower became known as Marten's Tower.

Throughout his lengthy period of 'house arrest' Marten lived in comparative comfort with his wife and daughters, occupying a suite of rooms and attended by his own staff of servants. He was granted many privileges: allowed a plentiful supply of money, receive friends and visitors and journey throughout the neighbourhood. Clearly, Henry Marten was no dungeon prisoner!

Moreover, he was able to carry on the writing of which he was fond. In 1662 he wrote 'Henry Marten's Familiar Letters to his Lady of Delight'. Within its pages he incorporated various letters written to his mistress, Mary Ward; the expletives of affection demonstrate that Marten was not the strict moralist he purported to be in public life. Even his biographer candidly states that 'he was a great lover of pretty girls, to whom he was so liberal that he spent the greatest part of his estate on them'.

Having had ample time to reflect upon his journey through life, Marten cleverly composed his own

acrostic epitaph using his name as the first letter of each line reading downwards. He died suddenly on 9th September, 1680, aged 78 years and was laid to rest in nearby St. Mary's Parish Church. The simple tombstone inscribed with his own epitaph reads as follows:

Hear or elsewhere (all's one to you and me)
Earth, air or water gripes my ghostless dust,
None knows how soon to be by fire set free;
Reader, if you on oft-try'd rule will trust,
You'll gladly do and suffer what you must.

My time was spent in serving you and you
And Death's my pay it seems, and welcome too;
Revenge, destroying but itself, while I
To birds of prey leave my old cage and fly;
Examples preach to th' eye-care then (mine says)
Not how you end, but for how you spend your days.

Even in death Henry Marten gained no everlasting peace. A bigoted 18th-century cleric named Thomas Chest objected to the presence of the grave in the chancel; he piously maintained that Marten was unworthy of so hallowed a spot. Accordingly, the regicide's bones were exhumed and reinterred under the floor of the entrance vestibule where they remain to this day - hidden from view under a carpet! Upon the vicar's death his son-in-law, Mr. Downton, satirised him thus:

> *Here lies at rest, it is confest,*
> *One chest within another.*
> *The chest of wood was very good,*
> *But who says so of t'other?*

The days when Chepstow Castle witnessed bloody battles and political intrigue are long gone. Marten's Tower lies in ruins and floorless; the open cellar, three storeys, the small chapel and evidence of mighty fireplaces confirm that Marten did not live in squalor.

It is difficult to understand how a man such as Henry Marten, a typical Revolutionary, survived virtually unscathed in an age of treachery, deceit and barbarism. That he was a political manipulator centuries ahead of his time cannot be doubted. In any age, such men of outstanding oratory and vision are indeed rare. Perhaps that is just as well.

All At Sea

During February 2000 a fine new hospital opened on the outskirts of Chepstow in the Five Acres field alongside St. Lawrence Road; a purpose built 84-bed, state-of-the-art centre designed to serve the medical needs of the local community well into the new millennium.

But what puzzles many patients and visitors alike is the seemingly incongruous massive stone Admiralty crest displayed beside its entrance. Herein lies a story unfamiliar to the present generation.

The current hospital stands on the site of the former Mount Pleasant Hospital, which was built in 1917-18 by the Admiralty for workers at Chepstow's bustling National Shipyard and their families. However, in 1919 it was taken over by the Ministry of Pensions for ex-servicemen of the First World War suffering from the dreadful effects of 'gas' and other permanent disabilities. With the passing years the hospital became used for general surgery and the care of geriatric patients. Due to its outmoded facilities and state of disrepair Mount Pleasant was closed in 1995 and demolished.

There were fears that the impressive crest which fronted the old hospital would be lost forever. But not so. Pressure from the local history society secured its preservation and relocation; also, three multi-coloured stained glass windows - of Jesus Christ, St. Lawrence and St. Luke - which are incorporated within the new facility.

The Admiralty crest is an enduring reminder that a century ago shipbuilding flourished on the banks of the Wye and that the notion of 'health care' is not entirely new.

Bridge Of Hope

Since the opening of the M4 motorway the 'old' main road linking Newport and Cardiff has remained a largely picturesque and little-used route. But this has changed in sudden and dramatic fashion. For with the recent arrival to the area of the giant Korean electronics and semi-conductor company LG (who, incredibly, chose this corner of South East Wales as the base for its future European operations), the sprawling hamlet of Coedkernew has witnessed massive and traumatic changes. Here, in particular, the road network has undergone major redevelopment.

Spanning the dual carriageway of the newly realigned A48 'southern distributor road' stands an imposing modern steel footbridge of substantial proportions. Erected in 1997 and costing around £500,000 (funded jointly by the local authority and the Welsh Office), it replaces an earlier mundane structure made obsolete by the trunk road changes. Its imaginative outline dominates the landscape in the Coedkernew area of the Gwent Levels, a land area for centuries populated sparsely with but a few farmsteads and cottages.

The 120-ton bridge, although officially designed by Gwent Consultancy, is very much the brainchild of Ronald Yee, an architect renowned for many innovative international bridge designs. In the form of a trapezoidal box with spiral approach ramps at either end (which mirror Oriental motifs), the bridge spans a width of just over 81 feet; its towering arch tapers from its bases to its apex some 60 feet or more above the carriageways far below; in total its length is 182 feet.

With its imaginative design - and with more than a touch of the Orient - its futuristic appeal is obvious. Its sweeping arch links the past with the future, courageously spanning the worlds of the East and West, a tangible sign, a gateway to an exciting new era of co-operation between vastly differing cultures.

The old key industries of coal, iron and steelmaking which began the Industrial Revolution and which sustained the growth of the region until recent times are largely gone; the old certainties have been overthrown in spectacular fashion!

Yet this small part of Gwent can now proudly boast to be home to the latest advances in world silicon-chip technology, a technology befitting the 21st-century. Hence, this new footbridge is a potent symbol of success, raising the aspirations and expectations of the people of Gwent for an eagerly sought after level of economic and social prosperity.

Gone - But Not Forgotten

The village of Crumlin is best remembered for its once majestic railway viaduct, the most famous viaduct in the whole of South Wales. In its heyday, it was reputed to be the largest railway bridge in the world constructed wholly of lattice ironwork. Probably so. Certainly, it spanned the steep-sided and thickly wooded Ebbw Valley at a height of over some 200 feet and originally carried the Taff Vale Extension of the Newport, Abergavenny & Hereford Railway westward from Pontypool to Quakers Yard in Glamorganshire. In later years the route became part of the Great Western Railway network.

Crumlin Viaduct was designed by T.W. Kennard (who was associated with the Blaenafon Company) and extended to 1,650 feet long, supported about its midway by a natural spur of rock. Work on the massive project began in December 1853 with the laying of the foundation stone of the first pier in the middle of the old canal to Newport by Lady Isabella Fitzmaurice. Construction took $4^{1}/_{2}$ years to complete; the wrought iron used in its assembly was forged at Garnddyrys Ironworks near Blaenafon.

After a series of 'running trials' the Government Inspector declared the viaduct safe for public transport. The grand opening ceremony took place on Whit Monday, 1st June, 1857, and was witnessed by some 20,000 people. The viaduct was bedecked from top to bottom with bunting and 'guns' were fired continually throughout the day. Even a commemorative medal was struck to celebrate the auspicious occasion.

And for long afterwards, people journeyed from far and wide on special excursion trains to Crumlin to witness at first-hand the showpiece of the railway network, the lace-like viaduct, 'light and delicate as if it were the work of the fairy Ariel'.

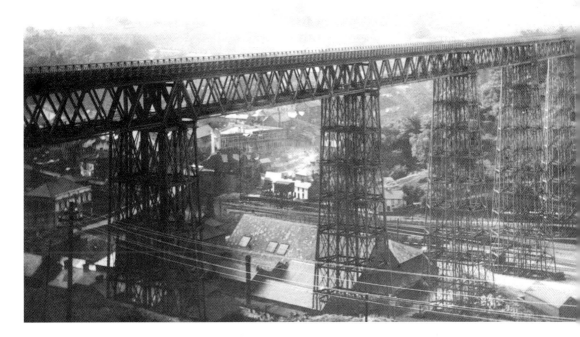

For years, travellers and locals alike were allowed to tread the wooden walkway beneath the rails, there to contemplate stupendous views of the surrounding hillsides and the glistening waters of the River Ebbw far below; also, the trains of the Western Valleys Railway running directly beneath the airy yet solid metal structure.

Gradually, the viaduct became an integral and accepted part of the landscape. Sadly, though, after just over 100 years in daily operation this engineering wonder of Victorian ingenuity was destined for the scrapyard's torch.

Why? With the demise of branch lines in England and Wales during the much maligned Dr. Beeching era (for such wanton vandalism the honourable gentleman was duly rewarded with a peerage by a grateful government!), the viaduct had outlived its usefulness. Amazingly, no authority was prepared to accept financial responsibility for its preservation and upkeep; thus, in 1966 the structure was unceremoniously demolished leaving the valley bereft of its outstanding landmark.

Ironically, the viaduct's greatest days of publicity came when it appeared in the 1960s blockbuster film, *Arabesque*, featuring Hollywood stars Gregory Peck and Sophia Loren making their breathtaking ride on horseback across the bridge in the most thrilling and spectacular sequence of the escapade.

Nowadays, Crumlin remains a sleepy backwater with little to belie its past. However, the elegant and graceful spectacle for which Crumlin was renowned is graphically recalled locally in a colourful mosaic along with other reminders of the area's history, such as the derelict red-brick surface buildings of nearby Navigation Colliery and the abandoned western arm of the Monmouthshire canal system. Yes, Crumlin still retains some vestiges of its industrial past.

A Plastics Brewery

In former days Gwent possessed a large number of local breweries, each producing its own distinctive range of traditionally brewed cask ales. Sadly, times have changed; nowadays beer-drinkers are offered mainly fizzy and bland ales produced by national commercial empires. The original valley brewhouses are a distant memory to all but a few.

However, at Cwmafon, between Pontypool and Blaenafon, the former brewery building of Westlake's has somehow managed to survive - as home to a thriving plastics factory!

In 1884 Charles Westlake purchased the Cambrian Brewery of Blaenafon which had begun brewing in the early 1880s. In 1889 he established Westlake's Brewery Limited. Yet from the outset Charles realised that the water supply at Blaenafon was unreliable. Hence a move down the valley to a well-watered site was essential for commercial viability.

The massive, five-storey tower brewhouse was constructed at Cwmafon in 1900 by leading brewery architects, George Adlam & Sons of Bristol: at the time it was the pinnacle of brewery design, both scientifically and practically.

The 'Nourishing Ales brewed from best quality materials and pure rising spring waters' alongside the Afon Llwyd at Cwmafon were highly regarded throughout the valley and won many prestigious awards during the early years of the past century. A rare poster from 1910 is still on display at the Whistle Inn at Garn-yr-Erw.

In 1911 the company took over the Castle Brewery, Pontypool and acquired their tied estate. However, following the First World War the demand for ale slumped drastically and brewing at Cwmafon ceased in 1928. Westlake's merged with Daniel Seys Davies' Reform Brewery of Abersychan. Surprisingly, the name of Westlake's continued to be used on draught and bottled ales.

In 1935 the brewery buildings were taken over by the Eastern Valley Subsistence Production Society to provide work for the unemployed during the Depression; no wages were paid for food production, clothing and agriculture, but the goods produced were sold very cheaply to the workers.

In 1939 the Reform Brewery was taken over by Andrew Buchan's of Rhymney and subsequently closed. A nearby pub still bears the name, the Westlake Arms: inside it displays a copy of the 1910 advertising poster.

In 1997 the Welsh Historic Monuments Agency, CADW, gave the former Westlake's Brewery a Grade II listing, describing it as 'A scarce, surviving example of a grand Victorian brewery in Wales, built by notable brewery architects and highly regarded at the time of construction'. Sadly, the once proud cathedral of beer stands forlorn, a symbol of a dream never realised.

Down On The Farm

The creation of the modern township of Cwmbrân has been an unqualified success. How refreshing, therefore, to find within this sprawling urban development an area that reflects a more leisurely and rural way of life.

Greenmeadow Community Farm was set up in the early 1980s by a group of local people determined to protect one of the last 'green' areas in Cwmbrân from residential or commercial development. Opened to the public in April 1991 and based around a white-washed 17th-century farmstead, the 150 acres site forms a 'green' horseshoe around the neighbouring housing estates. The farm has much to offer the entire family. After all, how many of today's children brought up on a diet of television, videos and computer games have ever come face-to-face with a live chicken, a duck, a goat, or a sheep, or even a cow in its natural habitat? The same may be said of a great many adults.

The range of animals on view is impressive; from traditional farmyard animals to the rarest of breeds. Within the cow shed there are daily displays of milking a cow. And at Pets Corner - always a favourite with the children - visitors are encouraged to handle and feed the smaller animals. Outside, the llamas remain a popular attraction with their cheeky food-grabbing antics.

Traditional country crafts feature prominently on the farm. In the workshops local craftsmen and women regularly demonstrate the centuries-old skills of the smithy, the farrier, spinners and weavers, amongst others.

The ancient stone barn offers a fascinating array of temporary and permanent exhibitions intended to enlighten those unfamiliar with the lore of the countryside. Naturally, the barn has its own barn owl and baby chicks.

The farmhouse tea rooms serve traditional Welsh home-made fayre; those with a raging thirst may enjoy a refreshingly cool glass of ale in the Sheep Dip Bar.

Anyone seeking a quiet ramble through unspoilt countryside will delight in the extensive woodland trail with its spectacular views across the Valley of the Crow and beyond to the gleaming Severn Sea; from fallow deer to green woodpeckers, a profusion of spring flowers, autumn fungi and winter buds, there is ample to captivate and satisfy those attuned to the world of nature and the

countryside. A large wild fowl area and ponds create a haven for rare migratory and over-wintering birds - a must for all bird-lovers.

Greenmeadow Community Farm, a magnificent rural retreat within a grey urban setting, continues to be one of Wales' top twenty tourist attractions welcoming over 100,000 visitors annually. And deservedly so! For whatever the season of the year there is always something new and exciting to appreciate. The farm is no show-piece farm - it really is a working farm. As such it provides a rich educational resource for the children and adults of the Eastern Valley and, equally, for those living outside the area. Indeed, the farm is the focus for much of the environmental activity in and around Cwmbrân Town.

Without doubt, the Community Farm is one of the finest of its kind - and is unique in the whole of Wales. Open everyday throughout the year, the farm offers 'Farm fun - for everyone'. Delightful!

The Square

Set high on the steep slopes of Mynydd Maen and overlooking the modern town of Cwmbrân is the isolated hamlet of Upper Cwmbrân. Nowadays, the hub of activity centres in and around The Square, a collection of neat rows of stepped, white-washed, terraced cottages built around the middle of the 19th-century to house the coalminers working in the nearby drift mines. The Square has remained largely unaffected by modern urban growth.

Here is the original Cwmbrân, or Cwmbrâen, long before the need to distinguish 'Upper' from 'Lower'. Little is known about its early history. It was once part of the Manor of Edlogan. During Norman times it was probably part of the Welshry. This upland area was better suited to pastoral farming than to the cultivation of crops, which remains true to this day.

Coal outcrops in the area were recognised and worked many centuries ago, chiefly by the monks of Llantarnam Abbey. By the beginning of the 17th-century, Upper Cwmbrân was the centre of a thriving if somewhat scattered village community with its own mill (referred to in 1610 as 'Melyn-y-vran'). The potential of the coal-stock embedded in the mountainside was realised by Major John Hanbury who acquired Thomas Arnold's small-scale 'Colework' in 1698 and expanded operations. By the middle of the 18th-century the mine was supplying coal to the tin works at Caerleon and Ponthir.

Further investment in the area began in earnest in 1793 when Thomas Stoughton, who married into the already wealthy Hanbury family, decided upon a major expansion of the existing workings. Porthmawr Colliery or the 'Clay Level' was opened nearby in 1837. The Mine Slope workings were opened in 1854.

Along with increased coal extraction, the need for suitable housing for the mine-workers became essential. Hence the building of Incline Row, Mine Slope Cottages and The Square. The rectangular layout of the Square was certainly unusual and, reputedly, based upon a Continental design. Hereabouts, the mountainside abounds with old quarry workings; the local freestone proved a convenient and durable material for the building of the cottages in The Square, other buildings and nearby farmsteads.

The spoil from the coal workings was literally thrown down the mountainside. After so many years, these waste tips have become overgrown with bracken and are hardly visible.

A curiosity of the early mine-workings was the creation of a tunnel driven all the way through the mountainside to Pontypool which, so the story goes, was used regularly by women wishing to shop in the nearby town.

With the start of iron-making in the valley below, the need for coal was imperative. The Upper Cwmbrân workings sent coal down by tramroad to fire the furnaces. Oddly, the iron-workers considered themselves superior to the miners - and shunned them accordingly.

During its heyday, more than one hundred children received their basic schooling at The Square in a large upstairs room above the Squirrel Inn (long since in ruins). Established in 1852 by local people with the help of the mine-owners, the 'School' lasted until 1868 when an imposing Victorian school building was opened at the lower end of Upper Cwmbrân.

The community also had its own brickworks, lime kilns, woollen factory, shop, post office, inns and chapels. (The latter exist still.) Yes, a flourishing community.

After a hard day's toil at the coal-face, no doubt the miners frequented the ancient Queen Inn, there to relax and quaff pints of foaming ale and share the day's experiences with friends.

A short distance from The Square, the silver-voiced stream of Nant Brân cadenzas its way down the cwm, unculverted, to the valley floor, spilling its sparkling waters into the fast-flowing Afon Llwyd.

The Square survived virtually unaltered until the 1960s when the local council, intent on eradicating the entire ancient settlement, began to demolish individual properties. However, the fiercely independent community protested vehemently and eventually the council gave way.

Today, the residents of The Square and Upper Cwmbrân tenaciously prize their independence and separate identity. And it is to be hoped that such a strong community spirit will last for many years to come.

On The Shoulders Of Giants

There is a giant in Cwmbrân. Really. No, not the rampaging, mythological, Celtic warrior, Brân. Rather a slender 8 feet 6 inches - tall giant standing in the Water Gardens opposite Monmouth Square - and definitely friendly.

The work of the Gower-based sculptor, Peter Nicholas, is very much a 'Millennium Statement'. The figure carrying a young child on his shoulders appears to be stepping out of the water and striding purposefully towards the town centre. The head of the child is impressed into the adult as on a coin and clearly represents the fusion of the future with the past: both are indivisible. Without doubt, a very powerful statement about the nature of human life itself.

The statue was commissioned by, and presented to, the people of Torfaen by the Cwmbrân Arts Trust with generous funding from local commerce. The 'surreal' sculpture was unveiled on 18th September, 2000, by Lord Raglan, and has since won public acclaim. Such a response is fully justified.

Incidentally, Sir Isaac Newton (1642-1727), generally acknowledged as the world's greatest man of science said: 'We are standing on the shoulders of giants.' (Examine carefully the inscription on the edge of a current £2 coin.) He was not referring to 'giants' of physical stature, but to men of incredible intellectual ability and foresight;

those who have influenced our perception of the world we inhabit. Put simply, his 'giants' were men of genius like himself, men of immense imagination and vision. For it is in no small measure that because of such 'giants', man has progressed from his primeval state to the civilisation of today.

The Cwmbrân Giant is no enigma; it is an icon strikingly fashioned in bronze. Moreover, it is a most welcome and eye-catching addition to the inferior works of art which 'enhance' an otherwise sterile and totally lacking in character town centre. It is the inspiration of a true modern visionary artist. Splendid!

A Story To Tell

Cwmbrân can boast a fine modern tile and mosaic mural reflecting the roots of the 'new town', which celebrated 50 years of age in 1999. Displayed prominently in Monmouth Square opposite the attractive Water Gardens, the huge mural is both exciting and adventurous in its conception. It comprises a series of colourful images designed and produced by children from the local primary and secondary schools: the work was co-ordinated by staff at Llantarnam Grange Arts Centre. Even the gymnasium, Justes Knecht, from Bruchsal in Germany, Cwmbrân's twinning town for over 20 years, contributed to the work.

Individual scenes depict the long defunct mining industry and ironworks, Llantarnam Grange, The Square at Upper Cwmbrân, church and chapel, boating lake, the modern housing stock, and former transport links by rail and waterway.

The sections were skilfully brought together to present a work of memorable quality. The mural was formally unveiled on 18th June, 1999, by Alun Michael, the then Secretary of State for Wales, in the presence of local dignitaries and pupils from the schools involved in the project. The energetic marching band, Fanfarenzug Bruchsal, added musical flamboyance to the occasion.

In today's climate where indifference and apathy are rife, it is gratifying that youngsters should enthuse over the creation of an unique work of art charting the social and industrial heritage of the lower Afon Llwyd Valley. But just how meaningful are past events to such juveniles? That's hard to say.

44

Drive To Another World!

For those anxious to escape the hurly-burly of modern urban life an outing to Cwmcarn Scenic Forest Drive offers a refreshing opportunity to savour the quietude of secluded woodland walks, experience the exhilaration of wonderfully bracing mountain air and to gaze at breathtaking views of the surrounding landscape.

At the foot of the Forest Drive the visitor centre houses many fascinating exhibits of the local flora and fauna; also, where information about the various walks can be collected. Throughout the year the centre hosts a varied programme of guided walks, demonstrations and events, such as wool spinning, lace work and embroidery, flower craft, wood turning, walking-stick cutting, the art of bonsai, pottery, displays of unusual snakes and other reptiles - and even clog and Morris dancing. Yes, something to suit just about every interest.

The centre has a gift shop amply stocked with local handicrafts and souvenirs; refreshments and snacks are readily available. Incidentally, nestling alongside the babbling waters of the Nant Carn brook is a well-appointed campsite for tents and touring caravans - an ideal base from which to explore South East Wales.

Leaving the centre the 7-mile signposted Forest Drive (the first of its kind in the entire country) sinuously winds it way through the valley of Cwm Carn, past Scots pine, Japanese larch, Sitka spruce and naturally grown deciduous trees. The latter provide a wonderful haven for wildlife, notably pigeons and green woodpeckers. The

timber felled was formerly used underground as pit props in the local collieries. Cwmcarn Colliery, which once dominated the scene hereabouts, has long gone and the valley has been transformed by reclamation and afforestation.

At focal points along the Scenic Drive huge wooden sculptures depict characters from the Celtic folklore stories of the Mabinogion. Each is expertly carved from a single block of seasoned oak by local artist John Hobbs; collectively, they truly seem to represent 'a self-guided story walk' in wood.

From the valley floor the route meanders tortuously ever upwards towards the mountain-top, past picnic areas, barbecue hearths and places for children's frolics. There are several car parks from which to admire the fabulous scenery or, for the more adventurous, to set off on walkabout.

Yet the highlight of the Scenic Drive must surely be to alight at Car Park 7 and make the short but strenuous ascent on foot to the ancient mystical tumulus of Twm Barlwm, a much-loved landmark upon the bare shoulder of Mynydd Maen, steeped in legend and romance, and where irrepressible skylark songsters spiral invisibly overhead.

From the summit the panorama is simply staggering. There can be no finer vistas in the whole of the County; southern Gwent and much of Glamorganshire are clearly visible, the glistening waters of the Severn Sea, Steep Holme and Flat Holme; in the distance the shadowy Somerset Mendips; inland the hills of northern Gwent and beyond the mysterious Black Mountains of Mid Wales.

Before returning to the valley floor far below and journeying homeward, what could be more delightful than to linger on the mountaintop, there to bask in the warm glow of a pleasant summer evening and watch the setting sun dip gently into the fathomless mountain ranges of South Wales. For such places evoke the tranquillity of timelessness. Marvellous.

The Village Schoolmaster

Devauden is a sleepy village set high on the ridge above Chepstow Park Wood, some 5 miles north-west of Chepstow. Yet behind its veneer of country respectability and quietude it can boast a fascinating history, especially in the field of education. For it was here that James Davies set about educating children in an age when 'learning' was the privilege of but a few. So what is the story behind the man whose devotion earned the respect of an archdeacon, a bishop, a Queen's Counsel and all who knew him?

James Davies was born the son of a farmer on 23rd August, 1765, at Blaen-Trothy, Llangattock-Lingoed, in the parish of Grosmont. Following his schooldays he joined a lawyer's office at Abergavenny, but disliked the daily tedium intensely - and ran away to Bristol. Sadly, he returned home with scarlet fever; his father became infected and died shortly afterwards; James, though, recovered fully.

He then became apprenticed to a weaver in nearby Grosmont, first working as a journeyman then as a masterman: this occupation lasted 15 years. In 1796 he made a disastrous marriage which remained childless. Following his wife's death, he moved to Usk where he set up business as a pedlar before opening a small shop in the town. Here he became acutely aware of the plight of the poor and needy - the very people he was destined to serve so tirelessly.

From this rather uncompromising background, and at the age of 45 years, he decided to become a schoolmaster. In 1812 he persuaded the authorities to found a school at Usk 'for the sons of the labouring poor who would be educated free' - with himself as the Headmaster. After a 'crash course' in schoolmastering at Abergavenny the Usk School was duly opened and proved extremely successful. In 1814 he decided to move to the remote hilltop hamlet of Devauden and establish there an Anglican School for secular and religious instruction.

And so the school where James Davies ate, slept and worked first opened its doors in June 1814. Within the schoolroom Davies took seriously his chosen task of

educating close to one hundred of 'the rude, ragged, boisterous mountain children' of Devauden. In 1830 a 'new' school was built alongside the original building.

Incidentally, whilst on the hilltop he never earned more than £20 a year, often considerably less. But he managed undeterred, working ceaselessly to help others in any way he could, even ministering to the sick and infirm. Much of his spare time was spent writing and issuing his own cogent moralising tracts.

Although a fair man, he would not tolerate indiscipline amongst his young charges. Persistently naughty children were placed in a wicker basket and hoisted up to the rafters of the schoolroom amid a tirade of verbal abuse and left to contemplate the error or their ways. Harsh treatment, perhaps, but surely effective.

James Davies held strong religious convictions. To fulfil his ambition for a church at Devauden, he devised novel fund-raising schemes including the collection of old rags to sell to a firm at Mounton. This earned him the nickname 'Jemmy the Rag', a name no doubt he bore with some pride.

In 1827 the ecclesiastical authorities licenced the schoolroom for evening services; the first full service was held before a congregation numbering over two hundred. In June 1836 the original school building was consecrated as a 'chapel of ease' within the parish of Newchurch - a dream come true for the ageing schoolmaster. (Only in 1958 was the chapel accorded the status of 'church', dedicated to St. James.)

In 1848, after 33 years at Devauden, James Davies left to take over mastership of the 'James Davies School' in the village of his birth. Shortly afterwards, though, he died on 2nd October, 1849, at the ripe old age of 84 years. He lies buried in the churchyard of Llangattock-Lingoed.

In 1986 the school he loved most was closed. Nowadays, the village children attend a modern, 'state-of-the-art' school at Shirenewton. Sadly, Devauden has lost its basic institution.

James Davies was undoubtedly a true humanitarian who cared deeply about his fellow men, a man universally loved and revered. He fervently believed that education and enlightenment should be freely available to all as a basic right whatever the circumstances. What he achieved at Devauden is surely testimony to the compassion and generosity of the human spirit. A pity, therefore, that in today's uncaring, grasping society the likes of such dedicated men are very rare indeed.

Fallen Upon Hard Times!

In a field on the western outskirts of Newport, overlooking the Wentloog Level and the Severn Sea, stands the remains of a once mighty cromlech, or ancient burial mound. For beside the bustling motorway at Cleppa Park, Duffryn, the semi-tumbled mass of huge grey stones provides a fascinating insight into how early man buried his dead.

After countless centuries of weathering the earth, stones and sods which formed the covering mound are all but gone. No doubt stones pilfered from the monument can be found embedded in the walls of nearby farm dwellings and out-buildings (a practice rife down the ages).

The tomb is probably some 4,000 years old and its construction must surely have posed considerable difficulties for Neolithic Man. What was the incentive for the early settlers to laboriously quarry and transport such massive blocks of siliceous sandstone to the site - and with little else than a handful of primitive tools? To honour the 'worthy' dead, probably. Yet the riddle remains lost in the mists of antiquity.

Several of the original supporting stones remain *in situ*. The gigantic capstone weighing several tons, though fragmented and fallen, rests wearily amongst the coarse grass of what was almost certainly a large chambered area; traces of a long mound survive still.

The tomb's design seems to have followed the influence of the Severn-Cotswold culture rather than the more westerly megalithic traditions of the Irish Sea, though this is open to conjecture. Like surviving relics elsewhere, its presumed alignment towards the Midwinter Sunrise point may be of significance, if only as an early indication of the ever-changing seasons.

The stones of Gwern-y-Cleppa are an emphatic reminder of pre-history; they bear mute testimony to the masters and craftsmen of a simple yet impressive technology, much concerned with symbolism, fertility and death. As such they are a worthy tribute to Man's imperishable faith in the immortality of the human spirit. Nowadays, though, these 'stones' lie largely ignored by historians and shunned by the public. Sadly, in all respects they have indeed fallen upon 'hard times'.

Bloomin' Lovely

Ebbw Vale was once home to a proud and thriving steel industry. That is now long past. Yet in the summer of 1992 the former 'steel town' was host to the Garden Festival of Wales. And what a spectacular success it proved to be. Thousands of people from all over the world daily thronged the Festival Site, appreciative of its landscaped beauty and multifarious attractions.

Thereafter, the vast site received little media attention. However, unlike former 'host' sites throughout Britain, often abandoned to become derelict, this Festival Site has been steadily transformed into a vibrant, modern village community.

And during October 1999, Victoria Village, just south of the town's main shopping thoroughfare, and consisting mainly of festival site houses, beat off stiff competition from the rest of Britain to be awarded the prestigious title of the UK's most blooming urban community by a panel of knowledgeable and experienced judges.

The challenge of the Britain in Bloom competition is to encourage urban communities to maintain their areas free of environmental problems such as litter, graffiti, dog fouling and the dumping of household waste; also to enhance such areas with sustainable horticulture. Victoria Village successfully realised these ideals. And far more. The judges commented: 'Where steel was once made, now wonderful displays of flowers grow... The hanging baskets and tubs were a delight...' The Keep Wales Tidy judges were highly impressed with the standard of cleanliness.

Victoria's path to glory began several years ago when the village won the regional competition through the sustained efforts of the entire community: this provided the impetus to compete nationally.

Not surprisingly, previous winners of the award have enjoyed substantial business opportunities. Victoria Village is no exception, having already benefited from its success. For nearby on the hillside overlooking the new community is Festival Shopping Park. This large retail site, based upon the American concept of 'outlet shopping', and the first to be established in Wales, is home to numerous shops selling well-known high-street brands and designer labels at discount prices; it attracts shoppers from miles around.

Victoria Village and those who today reside there can feel extremely proud of their achievement in such a demanding competition. Furthermore, the Village with its beautiful and tranquil lake setting is a role model for communities elsewhere to follow. Yes, and this in an industry-scarred valley town of Northern Gwent. Incredible!

The Putchers Of Goldcliff

Man has fished the waters of river and sea since the dawn of antiquity - largely out of necessity for sustenance. And at the scattered coastal village of Goldcliff on the Caldicot Level, renowned long ago for the splendour of its golden cliffs, golden sands, and Benedictine Priory (alas, these are no longer apparent), the ancient practice of catching salmon in 'putchers' continues to this very day at the local fishery.

Curiously, the right of fishing at Goldcliff was given to Eton College when it was founded during the reign of Henry VI. And the original line of 'putchers' dates back to 1442. It is further reputed that one day annually the fishery was expected to send enough salmon to satisfy the needs of the whole college. Though ownership has changed down the centuries, this ancient fishery with its unique method of fishing remains a viable commercial venture.

So what is so unusual about its way of catching fish? And what is a 'putcher'? The method entails stout wooden frameworks built across the main tidal flow of the murky waters of the Severn Estuary, each carrying row upon row of large cone-shaped baskets, or 'putchers'. The traditional putcher was between 5 and 6 feet in length and had staves and banding of willow branches cut from a 6-acre withy plantation at nearby Llanwern.

The dramatic ebb and flow of the Severn enables a large number of putchers to be submerged in serried 'ranks', around 2,000 in total. The unsuspecting salmon swimming a foot or two beneath the surface of the incoming tide enter the baskets: unable to swim backwards against the surging tide they become trapped and are left stranded with the ebbing tide. Easy catch!

The salmon season starts in May when the putchers are 'set'; they are left in place until August. Since 1952 the wooden putcher has given way to baskets constructed of more durable salt-resistant aluminium wire. Yet the medieval method of catching salmon at Goldcliff has hardly changed with the passage of time. Moreover, such a mode of entrapment bears silent testimony to man's ability and ingenuity to adapt and exploit the natural resources of his native environment.

An authentic wooden putcher mounted alongside a photographic display of Goldcliff Fishery can be viewed in Newport Museum. Fascinating.

Goytre Wharf

'Just messing about on the river.' A well-known song, certainly. But that is precisely what any 'water-man' can enjoy on the canal at Goytre Wharf, situated a little way off the main Abergavenny to Pontypool road above Llanofer Village.

Although known as the 'Mon & Brec', this stretch of waterway was originally the 'Brecknock and Abergavenny Canal', joining the now derelict Monmouthshire Canal at Pontymoile Basin. And it remains a fitting testament to the determination and engineering skills of Thomas Dadford Jnr, one of Britain's most successful canal builders, that he was able to route the winding 33-mile canal from Pontymoile around mountainous terrain and over gorges high above the Usk Valley to Brecon itself - with only a mere six locks to impede progress. Moreover, the entire canal and all its associated earthworks were 'raised' by hand using little more than picks and shovels; no mechanical aids were available to the early canal builders. The completed route was opened in 1812.

Man-made navigations were constructed specifically for transporting goods and minerals to sea-ports and other commercial outlets: they were very much the life-blood of the Industrial Revolution. However, the 19th-century saw a soaring demand for 'the two great traffics of coal and iron'. The Mon & Brec simply could not cope with the sheer volume of traffic. Too much moving too slowly. This did not please the grasping iron-masters whose wealth depended upon the rapid delivery of 'goods'. With the advent of steam locomotion (railway policy was 'to drive the traffic from the water to the rails'), the canal's future as a freight carrier was inevitably bleak.

By 1860 the canal was all but redundant. Whilst never a great financial success, without its availability and its link with the Monmouthshire Canal (opened in 1798) early industry in the nearby Eastern Valleys and the emerging port of Newport could never have developed so rapidly and prospered.

With generous financial help from Brecon and Gwent County Councils the old Brecknock & Abergavenny has been revitalised and is navigable from Sebastopol, just outside Pontypool, to the head of the canal at Brecon. Nowadays, the waterway is used extensively for boating excursions with small craft and motorised narrow boats slipping gently through its crystal waters.

The canal has many notable features, such as original warehouses, a tunnel, well-kept hump-back stone bridges each clearly numbered, wooden lift bridges, and an exceptionally well-preserved aqueduct at Brynich which carries the canal over the River Usk. The old limestone kilns at Goytre Wharf, once used to convert local stone into lime for building and agricultural purposes, have also been renovated. First fired in 1812, and set in a hollow some 30 feet below the waterway, they too are a reminder that the 'Mon & Brec' was indeed a working canal.

Probably the most impressive long boat to currently ply the canal is the 'Lord William De Braose'. Custom-built for canal cruising and based at the wharf, it offers relaxing cruises the whole year round: alongside the nearby aqueduct the buildings of Red Line Boats (hire cruises) add character to the waterside scene.

Yes, there is much to appreciate at Goytre Wharf. For in a fast-moving world of continual change it is refreshing to occasionally step aside from an urban existence and contemplate a former and more leisurely way of life in which Time itself remains static. The canal remains idyllic in its rural state. There are extensive woodland walks,

a large marina and craft sales. The Waterways Information Centre offers literature about the canal's history and the activities of British Waterways.

And what could be more delightful than to cruise through some of the most beautiful scenery in Gwent, through woodland glades and lush verdant countryside? Surely an experience no visitor to the 'Mon & Brec' at Goytre Wharf can fail to appreciate and treasure. Wonderful.

A Tale Of Two Wives

In a peaceful cemetery at Llanfoist near Abergavenny, beneath the brooding slopes of the Blorenge, lies the remains of Alexander Cordell, well-known novelist of the 20th-century. But closer inspection of the grave lends a touch of the bizarre befitting the man admired by many and of whom countless stories have been told. For not one, but **two** separate headstones stand upon the grave. How did this strange situation come about?

The first headstone perpetuates the memory of Patrick Michael (Max) Donovan who died in 1960 at the relatively early age of 46 years; and his wife Donnie who died aged 80 years. For many years the couple lived in Abergavenny and were neighbours of the Cordell family; they were also the very firmest of friends. The second headstone is dedicated to Cordell himself, his first wife, Rosina... and to Donnie, his second wife.

Rosina's death in 1972 left Cordell heartbroken and disconsolate: she had been a faithful and devoted companion for many years, and a good mother to their daughter Georgina. Yet his close friend Donnie (who had lost her husband some 12 years earlier) was to prove an invaluable source of comfort and inspiration to the brooding author. Their ever-constant friendship blossomed into romance and the couple eventually married in 1973.

Cordell doted on his second wife. With her at his side, he regained his former sense of direction; often, he claimed that his later novels were written especially for her. Certainly, these works display the heartfelt emotions of a tender and passionate man. After more than 20 years of happiness together Donnie, whose real name was Elsie, died in 1995. Thereafter, the great writer lost his zest for life - and writing.

Did Cordell have a premonition of his impending death? Probably so. Shortly before his demise he revisited Abergavenny specifically to arrange his own funeral. This he

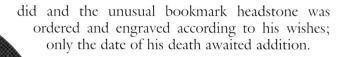

did and the unusual bookmark headstone was ordered and engraved according to his wishes; only the date of his death awaited addition.

After completing his final novel, 'Send Her Victorious', the 82 year-old Celyon-born author disappeared from his home in Rhosddu, Wrexham. Sadly, eight days later his lifeless body was discovered in a car near the Horseshoe Pass, Llangollen, his hands still clutching treasured family photographs: the author had died peacefully of natural causes.

To the end Cordell, whose real name was George Alexander Graber, was a pragmatist. He loved life and cared deeply about social injustice. After a humanist funeral service, his body was cremated and his ashes interred on the same day, the 9th July, 1997, alongside the remains of his two adoring wives and very close friend, Max.

The inscription on the bookmark headstone says of his wives:

> *AND*
> *BELOVED WIFE*
> *ROSINA*
> *WHO DIED*
> *20th MAY 1972*
> *The first, the loveliest*
> *and the best,*
> *and then came along*
> *DONNIE*
> *her friend;... to both*
> *wives I owe so much.*

And is it not perhaps ironic that Cordell's last resting place should not be faraway from that of Crawshay Bailey, the formidable and dynamic iron-master who during the Industrial Revolution brought much-needed prosperity to the County at the expense of the downtrodden working classes. From the iron-master and the bleak, forbidding countryside of northern Gwent, Cordell gleaned the inspiration for his most famous novel, 'Rape of the Fair Country'. First published in 1959, this powerful story set around the Blaenafon area during its heyday has sold millions of copies worldwide - and continues to be as popular as ever. A coincidence? Who can say!

Festive Cheer!

As elsewhere in Britain, Gwent is a county steeped in ancient beliefs, customs and superstitions; some of these have survived to enrich contemporary life. The origins of such ritual observances are obscure, lost forever in the grey mists of antiquity. Nonetheless, the people of Gwent have long celebrated the months of the year with a varied and often elaborate system of time-honoured rites.

One such tradition associated with Christmas is the Mari Lwyd; this survived in rural areas of eastern Gwent until quite recently. The Mari Lwyd means 'Grey Mare' (as in nightmare). Traditionally, this was a horse's skull carefully cleaned, bleached white and mounted upon a wooden pole. If no such skull was readily available a carved block of wood would suffice. The large eye-holes were stuffed with wadding until they bulged outwards in gruesome fashion. The ears were fastened on by the young girls of the household to resemble a startled animal's ears; the nostrils were filled like 'those of the horse as if using the sense of smell, in his eagerness, to discover what had startled him'. The lower jaw was fitted with a spring and a cord which, when abruptly pulled, caused an awful grating sound or 'snap'. The horse's head was decorated with brightly coloured ribbons, rosettes and bells, and the supporting pole draped with a long white sheet.

Throughout the Twelve Days of Christmas a large party of men took pleasure in parading the horse's head from household to household. The ritual began with the leader of the group (usually the eldest) rapping smartly upon the front door. The person bearing the horse's head then sang a rhyme in Welsh, whereupon an impromptu verse competition ensued between the 'horse' party and those within the house. Such necessary and amicable 'leg-pulling', or repartee, was known as 'pwnco'.

Eventually, this veritable 'battle of song and wit' came to an end, the Mari Lwyd and companions having proved themselves worthy of hospitality: the door was unbolted and the entire entourage welcomed inside, there to entertain and partake of good festive cheer. The Mari Lwyd would wildly skip and frolic and, to the delight of those looking on, chase after the young girls of the household in order to subdue and frighten them. The horseplay finally ended in dignified fashion with a 'step' or country dance.

The Mari Lwyd used to be a familiar sight all over South Wales. It was eagerly awaited and considered to be an essential part of the Christmas festivities. However, it was not welcomed everywhere. For those unaccustomed and unfamiliar with this most bizarre of Welsh customs, the spectacle of the Mari Lwyd would have been a most terrifying experience.

Inevitably, perhaps, with the decline of the Welsh language during the latter part of the 19th-century this curious and widespread custom all but died out. Yet in recent years several Welsh folk-dance groups delight in re-enacting and perpetuating this annual custom. A fine example can be witnessed at the isolated village of Llansoy in the Parish of Llanfihangel Tor-y-Mynydd. Yes, the Mari Lwyd is far from dead!

An emphatic reminder of this essentially Welsh custom can still be found at Llanofer, near Abergavenny. For mounted prominently above the entrance of the quaint old village post office a 19th-century framed painting (whose origin and precise date is uncertain) strikingly depicts the Mari Lwyd outside nearby Llanofer Hall. The building is dimly lit by the light of a crescent moon; a youngish man leading a white-clad figure wearing a horse's head approaches the door; in the background shadowy figures lurk menacingly.

Sadly, many of the ancient rites kept alive by our forefathers are largely forgotten now. A pity really for, like the Mari Lwyd, such rites reflect the imaginative mind and the mystical spirit of man. Without them our cultural and spiritual heritage would surely leave us all very much the poorer.

Llanyrafon Mill

On the outskirts of Cwmbrân, Llanyrafon Mill stands in a dilapidated state, abandoned and neglected for many years. Yet this formidable stone building has stood beside the waters of the Afon Llwyd for centuries. Water-mills were a common enough sight during the 17th-century, but with the advent of the Industrial Revolution most had outlived their usefulness and became derelict.

Documentary evidence proves that there was a mill on this site in 1632. And there is good reason to believe that the mill is considerably older. For on his map of 14th-century South Wales and The Borders, William Rees plots a 'Mill on Avon' - surely Llanyrafon Mill.

The mill belonged to the Manor of Edlogan which was owned by the Griffith family from the 1660s until 1880. Thereafter followed a succession of different owners and millers. During its working life the mill served a wide-ranging area; also it provided flour for several notable houses including Tredegar House, Newport, the home of the Morgan family.

Originally a three-storey corn mill powered by the huge waterwheel of the overshot type, it should really be called Llanyrafon Mills. Why? Simply because unlike the majority of mills found elsewhere which possess one set of grinding stones, Llanyrafon possesses **three** sets of massive grinding stones connected to the complicated mechanical gear.

Water is the 'life-blood' of any water-mill. This was drawn from the nearby river, Afon Llywd, about half a mile upstream and carried along a narrow, fast-flowing feeder stream at the correct height to turn the massive waterwheel. The miller was able to control the water level to the wheel by use of a lever which opened and closed the sluice gate in the trough. The existing trough replaced an earlier worn wooden one around 1920.

Like mills elsewhere, the miller allowed water to trickle constantly over the wooden blades of the wheel even when there was no milling in progress. This was to prevent the wood drying out and splintering, thereby ensuring its longevity. The present blades are of metal though they are badly affected by years of corrosion.

No doubt the mill has seen considerable alteration and modification down the years. Yet its basic structure remains very much the same as when it was first constructed.

Sacks of harvested grain brought to the mill were hoisted to the top floor and stored in large bins, or hoppers. Chutes led down to the grinding stones on the first floor, massive stones made of hard-wearing French burr. Following milling, the flour or 'meal' passed downward to the ground floor where it was bagged ready for despatch to the customer.

During the First World War the mill continued to grind vast amounts of flour. Apart from this period of necessity, it was mostly used for preparing animal feed. In 1945 an electric grinder was installed and used continually until the mill ceased operating in the early 1950s.

Thereafter, the mill was left to decay, to become covered with brambles and nettles. No-one seemed to care. But this was not so. For in December 1995 'The Friends of Llanyrafon Mill' was formed consisting of people interested in, and committed to, preserving the heritage of the area.

Fortunately, Llanyrafon Mill has passed into the ownership of Torfaen County Borough Council and has become a listed building. Undoubtedly, it is a building of historical importance. And it is to be hoped that within the next few years Llanyrafon Mill will be fully restored to a working facility.

Only when the waterwheel turns incessantly will the whole building come alive again, alive to the rumbling of the cogs and the lively chattering of the damsels, and the syncopated sound of water falling on to the wheel's broad blades - sounds of man attuned to nature and his environment.

Then, and only then, will future generations in the 'Valley of the Crow' be able to gain an enlightening glimpse of an almost forgotten way of rural life.

A Sobering Experience

In bygone days every village and town dispensed its own brand of justice to drunks, wrong-doers and petty criminals. One 'instant' form of punishment was an enforced spell in the local 'stocks' (a locked wooden framework with holes for the feet), whereby members of the public could ridicule and persistently pillory the person confined. Usually, this involved the miscreant being pelted with rotten eggs, fruit and vegetables. Ugh! No doubt, after such an unpleasant experience many culprits surely realised the error of their ways.

At Mitchel Troy beside the softly murmuring waters of the River Trothy, some 2 miles south-west of the famous market town of Monmouth, the village stocks stood for many years alongside the straggling highway to Raglan. However, after falling into disuse the remarkably well-preserved timber treble stocks were removed to a place of lasting safety - inside the Church of St. Michael where they are displayed to this very day.

It is interesting to speculate whether or not such forms of humiliation were more effective than the lenient sentences imposed upon current reprobates. Perhaps, herein lies a valuable lesson for modern-day society to ponder over. Nevertheless, the treble stocks must surely have many a colourful tale to tell.

The small yet pretty church, largely rebuilt on its Norman foundations but still retaining its pointed arches of the 13th-century, houses several fascinating artefacts. Most obvious, and preserved within the porch, is the roughly incised memorial stone to Phillip Stead, churchwarden, who died on 13th December, 1736, aged 67 years. The grammar may be rather weak, but the sentiment is clear:

Life is Unsartain
And Deth is so shuer
Sin is The Wound
& Christ is the Cuer

Surely, a tribute befitting a stalwart servant of the faith hereabouts.

In the rather austere nave stands an early 17th-century table, richly decorated with fluting and roundels, and with a brass plate delicately engraved with Christ at the Last Supper. A wonderful piece of artistry!

Outside, stands a massive old wooden lych-gate with an arched stone-tiled roof; and in the churchyard a 14th-century cross (without a cross!) has curious and much weathered dimpled ornamentation. Herein lies the resting place of Herefordshire parson, Thomas William Webb, a noted astronomer of his day: born at Ross-on-Wye in 1806, he was buried in 1885 beside his wife, Henrietta, in the village of her birth.

Yes, the church at Llanfihangel Troddi (its Welsh name is far more lyrical to the ear than its anglicised form) harbours much to greet the inquisitive visitor.

Gateway To The Past

Everyday, people who journey along the Pontypool to Usk highway pass through the inconspicuous village of Monkswood. Yet just off the beaten track and tucked away in a little-used country lane near Great Estavarney Farm is a most curious and unlikely relic of the British Empire - a pair of ornamental gates at the entrance to 'Three Springs', a private dwelling built and occupied by the late George Bailey.

Both gates bear an inscription. One has the following two lines of Latin text:

Forsan et haec olim meminesse juvabit.
Materiem superabat opus.

The first quotation is taken from Virgil's 'Æneid', the Roman epic poet's most famous and accomplished work: it translates as 'Perchance even this distress it will be a joy to recall some day'. The second phrase is derived from the Latin poet Ovid's 'Metamorphoses' and states quite simply 'And the workmanship was more beautiful than the material'. An appropriate sentiment.

The inscription on the companion gate is far more intelligible to the layman and self-explanatory:

This panel formed part of the P. (av)
ement at the Cornhill entrance
of the Royal Exchange, (London),
destroyed by fire 10th. January 1838.

Were these gates manufactured at a local forge? And how did they come to rural Gwent? According to the widow of George Bailey her daughter purchased the gates upon impulse in 1960 as a birthday present for her father whilst attending a sale of country 'wares' - in Oxfordshire. Her father proudly erected the unusual portals at the then family home.

It is somewhat incredulous that such an importance vestige of English heritage should find its way to such a quiet backwater as Monkswood. Yet, by contrast, how many cherished artefacts have left their native Welsh soil down the years to languish in some foreign land? Who can really say!

The Monmouth Cap

The historic market town of Monmouth has many claims to fame: the birthplace of a king, Henry V, a ruined castle, and a town full of character. Yet long ago the town was famous for something quite different - the celebrated Monmouth Cap.

Across the waters of the Monnow with its ancient fortified bridge, Overmonnow or Little Monmouth was originally a separate borough. In medieval times it was known as Cappers' Town, the centre of a flourishing industry that brought much fame and prosperity to Monmouth.

Undoubtedly, the most famous reference to these close-fitting caps is in Shakespeare's play 'Henry V', published ca.1599, when Captain Fluellen, referring to the Welsh bowmen at the Battle of Agincourt, said 'If your Majesties is remembered of it, the Welshmen did goot service in a garden, where leeks did grow, wearing leeks in their Monmouth caps, which, your Majesty knows to this hour is an honourable padge of service; and I do believe your Majesty takes no scorn to wear the leek upon St. Tavy's day'.

Interestingly, a price control was fixed by law in 1489 on hats and caps which said 'that no capper or hatter should sell any hat above 20 pence or cap above 2/8d'. Moreover, in 1523 one Thomas Capper leased a house in Monnow Street, presumably for the manufacture of caps. A few years later Monmouth's town charters mysteriously disappeared only for several of them to be discovered in a shop window where 'Thomas Capper used them instead of cloth to lay under his caps'.

In 1571 Elizabeth I decreed 'that every person, above 7 years of age, should wear on sabboth and holydays, a cap of wool, knit made, thickened and dressed in England, by some of the trade cappers...' The consequences of failing to obey the ruling was a hefty fine of 'ten groats for omission thereof'. Predictably, the edict was well received by the people of Monmouth who gave blessings 'to the kindly Queen' who brought much-needed work to the town.

Monmouth Caps held a wide appeal. Because of their durability and versatility, Francis Drake and Hawkins purchased some 36 dozen of the headwear for their last expedition. Even the armed forces wore them: in 1627 the Privy Council ordered 6,000 caps for 'land soldiers'. Cromwell recognised their worth by supplying his soldiers with them. Likewise, the Navy included them in its list of 'slop clothing' in 1660 and 1693.

But what did Monmouth Caps actually look like? They were close-fitting, round and made of wool in various colours with costly linings. A rare specimen thought to be either Elizabethan or a late 17th-century farm labourer's cap is displayed in the local museum. Though quite plain, it has a ribbed brim and a stocking-stitch top.

Thomas Fuller in 'The Worthies of England', 1662, described the caps enthusiastically as 'the most ancient, general, warm and profitable covering of men's heads in this island'.

Certainly, before the Black Death the capper industry was extremely wealthy; it possessed its own Cappers' Chapel in the church of St. Mary before it was pulled down in 1736. Fuller says 'The cappers' chapel doth still remain, being better carved and gilded than any other part of the church'.

But with the plague, cap-making in Monmouth came to an abrupt end. To escape the dreaded disease many workers fled northward to Bewdley in Worcestershire. Subsequently, the knitting of Monmouth Caps became commonplace elsewhere. It never returned to its home town - but the name Monmouth Cap survived.

What was special about Monmouth Caps? Well, for the very first time in Britain such 'clothing' was knitted from wool and not made from cloth or leather as was hitherto customary. Monmouth was a pioneer of the art of knitting; it reached the town from the continent some 30 years before it became popular elsewhere.

Curiously, the Monmouth Cap lives on. Isca Morrismen, a group dedicated to preserving the centuries-old tradition of The Morris, have long incorporated it into their individual costume or 'kit'. Copied from the specimen displayed in Monmouth Museum, the caps are an evocative reminder of Monmouth's former role in the history of fashionable 'dress'.

Strolling amongst the quaint and picturesque houses of Overmonnow, it is easy to visualise the 'cottage' industry where once workers toiled tirelessly to produce a peculiar yet distinctive 'head-gear' fit for a nation.

A Shot In The Dark

Monmouth can boast many hostelries of charm and character, each associated with an interesting tale or two. This is certainly true of the Queen's Head, a coaching inn over 350 years old near the Wye Bridge. For, reputedly, within this fine black-and-white timber-framed building an attempt was made on the life of no less a person than Oliver Cromwell!

During the Civil War the townspeople of Monmouth supported the Royalist cause. Despite much stubborn defence, the town and its beleaguered castle eventually succumbed to the more powerful Parliamentarian forces - the Roundheads. When Cromwell himself visited the town in May 1648 (some argue August 1646) and spent a night at the ancient inn he narrowly escaped assassination by a Royalist named Evans. Only the quick thinking of a local burgess saved the day by knocking upwards the cocked barrel of the musket aimed at Cromwell. An upstairs room - the Cromwell room - still sports bullet holes in its rafters.

It is also claimed that the ghost of the would-be assassin, or that of one of his fellow conspirators, 'a shadowy, vague figure', continues to haunt the inn. Why such visitations are frequently linked with injustices, violent deaths or, as in this instance, 'tasks left unfinished in life' provide much food for thought.

Did Cromwell really visit the Queen's Head Inn? Or was the abortive assassination attempt a mere fabrication by political opponents? Curiously, there is no mention of the incident by Cromwell's many English biographers. Neither do they even record his visit to Monmouth. To compound matters further, sources nearer to 'home' maintain that the attempt occurred a short distance away while Cromwell was dining at St. James' House in Whitecross Street, the home of the Fortune family. All most confusing. Nevertheless, the honour of harbouring Cromwell has long been bestowed upon the Queen's Head.

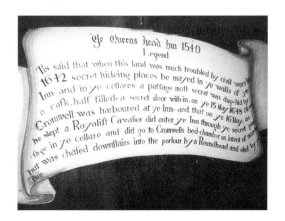

Whether true or otherwise, the foregoing story is certain to capture the imagination of those with a penchant for political intrigue. For what might have been the impact upon the political scene of England had the future 'Lord Protector' met an untimely death on the Welsh side of Offa's Dyke? If the attempt upon Cromwell's life had proved successful, it would surely have changed the whole course of British history. A most intriguing thought!

Harvest Of Souls

Set high above the Sirhowy Valley the straggling hamlet of Mynyddislwyn (Islwyn's Mountain) has splendid views of the surrounding landscape; and the church of St. Tudor has many fascinating stories to tell.

Surprisingly, the church is built on the brow of the mountaintop, not on the higher position of Mynydd-y-Lan. Why? Tradition has it that the early Christians built their first church overlooking a grove where pagan ceremonies were once held: they wished to worship the new-found 'God' in a fitting and proper manner. But on two separate occasions the building mysteriously collapsed at nightfall. Somewhat perplexed, the builders decided to keep vigil throughout the hours of darkness. And during the following evening they heard a celestial voice saying in Welsh, 'Myned is y llwyn, Myned is y llwyn', (Go below the bush, Go below the bush). The advice was heeded. The unholy spot was abandoned and the church was built in its present location - hence the name Myned-is-y-llwyn which eventually became corrupted to Mynyddislwyn.

Yet another version tells of a white-clad horseman carrying the building material taken there during the day farther down the mountainside, calling to the night sky 'I'r llwyn! I'r llwyn!', (To the grove! To the grove!).

St. Tudor's was granted 'church' status ca.1102 to Glastonbury Abbey, but later became affiliated with Llantarnam Abbey. The registers commence in the year 1664.

Due to centuries of weathering and neglect, the church was largely rebuilt in 1820 and remains a simple house of worship. A large painting, 'The Mockery Of Christ Crowned With Thorns', dominates the north aisle.

The tombstone of John Rees has markings resembling flagons and a domino. Yet the flagons are really chalices incised into the stone; the domino-effect is probably where six studs once held a brass memorial plate on the stone.

Within the churchyard several ancient yew trees have piles of stones around their bases as if to buttress them against the blustery winds that continually blow over this most windswept of mountains. And all around are the graves of sturdy stock who once daily farmed the mountaintop. Harvest of souls! These unknown peasants may have reaped no fame, yet they sleep in peace throughout the ever-changing seasons.

Many legends surround Mynyddislwyn, some perhaps more fanciful than others. According to one tradition (hard to believe!) St. Paul visited Britain during a missionary journey and preached hereabouts.

Alongside the churchyard is the ancient tumulus known as Twyn Tudur (Tudur was a Welsh saint). Contemporary sources state that deep within the mound lie the bodies of Roman soldiers slaughtered by Welshmen defending their territory. The remains of circular ditches and earthworks surrounding the massive 'tump' are still clearly visible.

Twyn Tudur has long been thought to contain buried treasure. Adventurers have attempted to delve into the heart of the tump with pick and shovel - only to be thwarted by sudden changes in weather; the skies clouding over followed by violent storms, the deafening rumbles of thunder and blinding flashes of lightning, sufficient to strike fear into any God-fearing soul. Terrified and believing some malevolent force was at hand, the treasure-seekers fled for their lives. Very sensible, too.

Until the late 19th-century, an early morning service was held in Mynyddislwyn on Christmas Day - the Plygain. This custom dated back to Roman Catholic, pre-Reformation times, if not even earlier. The church was lit by candles, each decorated meticulously around its lower part with hoops and coloured paper. Sadly, like many rural traditions, the 'Plygain' has vanished from the modern scene.

A practice peculiar to Mynyddislwyn was for the treatment of dog bites. Certain stones in the parish were called 'hydrophobia stones'. For anyone bitten by a mad dog the remedy involved grinding a piece of such stone into a fine powder and mixing with fresh milk before giving to the victim. Ah! Were mad dogs commonplace in the vicinity? Presumably so.

Incidentally, it was Islwyn, 'the Sweet Singer of Sirhowy', arguably Wales' greatest poet of the 19th-century, who took his bardic name from the mountain in whose shadow he lived.

Adjacent to St. Tudor's is the Church House, a hostelry that for centuries has quenched the thirsts of those attending the weekly services next door; also, to the farmers and friends who regularly meet after a hard day's work, there to relax and enjoy good ale and convivial conversation.

Many of the foregoing tales are without doubt highly colourful. Nonetheless, the mystical hamlet of Mynyddislwyn with its ancient church, inn and 'tump' are timeless gems in a materialistic world of constant change.

Gŵyl Werin Tŷ Tredegar
(Tredegar House Folk Festival)

In recent years there has been a resurgence of interest in traditional Folk Dance, Song and Music amongst an ever-widening cross-section of society. Nowhere is this more apparent than at the annual Tredegar House Folk Festival, Newport. Held during the middle of May in the picturesque grounds of one of the most magnificent Charles II stately homes in Britain, there could be no better venue as a showcase for the talents of dancers and musicians from the world over.

The festival began in 1989 from very modest beginnings, the brainchild of Marcus Butler, himself a highly talented concertina player. His business, Marcus Music, specialises in the making and repairing of traditional musical instruments and is housed in the restored block of craft workshops. His original idea was to establish a weekend festival with the emphasis on 'participation' rather than an 'appreciation'. This was readily achieved.

Since those early days of 'try-it-and see', the festival has grown in popularity and stature with each passing year. Long-supported by Newport County Borough Council, and with the financial aid of a small Arts Council grant, it finally achieved 'International Festival' recognition in 1996 when dance sides from outside Wales flocked to Tredegar Park to join local performers.

In 1998 the Festival celebrated its 10th anniversary - and received a National Lottery arts award. Commendation indeed. And deservedly so. Today, the Festival is truly international with dance teams travelling from all over Europe to perform their country's dance customs at Newport.

Such is the popularity of the event that there are numerous impromptu music and song sessions throughout the grounds, quite apart from the more formal concerts, ceilidhs, and dance workshops. And the workshops include American Line Dancing, Irish Set Dancing, even how to play the Didgeridoo; yes, the Festival seems to offer it all. And there is no

shortage of members of the public eager to join in and gain new experiences.

The 3-day event follows a well organised programme, beginning early on the Friday evening with an informal gathering in the brewhouse and courtyard where old acquaintances are renewed and new friendships forged. With seemingly limitless casks of real ale and cider 'on tap', it doesn't take long before all present are revelling in the spirit of the occasion.

Saturday is very much Dancers' Day with many of the sides dressed in spectacular costumes - a joy to behold, and greatly appreciated by the thousands of admiring onlookers. Amongst these displays, dance sides from local schools typify what the festival is all about - young and old enjoying themselves in the world of folk: their enthusiasm is infectious. An evening concert with well-known artists and an energetic ceilidh with a vibrant band rounds off the day superbly. The Sunday offers more of the same.

Unlike events elsewhere, entry into the grounds of Tredegar House remains free to the general public, courtesy of the generosity of the local council. Only the concerts, ceilidhs and workshops are ticketed events.

On a broader note, the site offers excellent camping facilities. Other diverse attractions include a craft market, boating on the lake, carriage rides, an adventure playground for children and, of course, the magnificence of Tredegar House itself. Yes, everything to satisfy the most discerning enthusiast.

In an age of materialism and disaffection, it is indeed heartening to find so many individuals who willingly give their time freely to perform and entertain; and whose only reward is the personal satisfaction gained from perpetuating centuries-old traditions of the music and dance cherished so dearly by our forefathers.

Tredegar House Folk Festival is a highly colourful and spirited celebration of traditional folk values. It's a hectic weekend. Agreed. And long may it continue so to do. An occasion not to be missed!

Newport Castle

Seen by so many - appreciated by so few. Yet Newport Castle, strategically situated on the banks of the surging waters of the River Usk, boasts a chequered and proud past. Though lacking the grandeur of Chepstow Castle, when viewed from the eastern bank of the river the castle at Newport remains impressive in its melancholy dereliction.

Whilst its early history is somewhat obscure, a motte and bailey castle was first established on Stow Hill overlooking the town by Robert Fitzhamon around 11000.

With the arrival of the railway in the 1840s, the last vestiges of this early Norman castle were obliterated by debris from the excavated railway tunnel far below.

During the 14th-century the Lordship of Newport passed through marriage to the Earls of Stafford. The present castle along-side the riverbank was founded by Earl Hugh probably between 1372 and 1386. He was intent upon stopping the constant raids by the Welsh: after all, the river was, and still is, fordable at low tide. Strangely, the side of the castle facing the town seems never to have been completed.

The building was further fortified between 1403 and 1406 during the insurrection led by Owain Glyndŵr. But to little avail. For the fiery Welsh chieftain and his men not only ransacked the town, but besieged the castle and destroyed much of it. The remaining structure was subsequently rebuilt and remodelled between 1424 and 1457 on the order of Humphrey Stafford, the first Duke of Buckingham, and his successors.

Newport Castle then passed into the hands of the Herberts for some 200 years. An attempt was made during the Civil War to garrison the castle for Charles I. But Colonel Herbert was forced to surrender it to Cromwell's troops. Its great days as a fortress were well and truly over.

Thereafter, unwanted and uncared for, the castle fell upon hard times and suffered many indignities. During the early 1800s it was home to a tannery with the apartments in the south tower used as storerooms and stables; from 1820 to 1899 it became the site for the breweries of Allfrey (1820), Searle & Herring (1880), and 10 years later Lloyd & Yorath, who in 1899 moved to larger premises in the town itself. Throughout this period the central tower was capped with a red-tiled roof. How incongruous that must have appeared! At the close of the 19th-century the ruins were acquired by Newport Corporation and Lord Tredegar.

The present building comprises three fragmentary towers linked by a short length of curtain wall and date from the 15th-century. Of particular interest is the massive central tower. For at basement level, and unique amongst the castles of Gwent, is a remarkable high-vaulted Water Gate, or dock. Though now choked with mud and debris, vessels bearing provisions once berthed here at high tide, protected by heavy double portcullises operated from the floor above. A survey of 1522 describes it as a 'a vawte or entre to receive into the said Castell a good vessell'.

In the spacious first-floor apartment known as the Presence Chamber, its superbly vaulted ceiling still crowned by a large double tudor rose surrounded by smaller single roses, former Lords of Newport sat on formal and ceremonial occasions. Little remains of the mighty Great Hall apart from its windows overlooking the river, together with the original fireplace. The top floor housed a chapel with a large east-facing window and was reached by a spiral stone staircase.

In 1930 the castle passed into State ownership and some conservation work was carried out. Safe at last it seemed. But not so. For in 1970 large parts of the northern corner were demolished to make way for a modern roadway - surely the ultimate in wanton vandalism!

Like ancient buildings elsewhere, Newport Castle is reputed to be haunted. The bearded ghost of its founder regularly roams the ruins only to vanish as soon as any mortal eye falls upon it. Those glimpsing the fiery giant's spectre describe it as a most terrifying experience. Interesting...

Without doubt, the once imposing stronghold of Newport Castle epitomises an age of biffer strife: it was a formidable bastion of authority and baronial power. Now it stands a long-forgotten, neglected and largely unseen monument to the Past.

The ruined castle is in the care of CADW, the Welsh Historic Monuments Agency, and is freely open to the public. Displayed prominently within its grounds is a die-cast model of the castle as it might have looked in 1450, together with a synopsis of its history.

Newport Market

Markets hold a strange fascination for the majority of people. Whether indoor or outdoor, they invariably draw the crowds eager for a bargain or simply good value for money. In Newport the oldest shopping experience is to be found at the impressive Victorian indoor market, opened on May Day 1889. Situated at the corner of High Street and Dock Street, its magnificent stone front looks out over the surging tidal waters of the nearby River Usk.

Surprisingly, perhaps, Newport Market has a centuries-old royal charter; a market was established here in the early 13th-century. Even today, there are many folk who consider the market to be one of Newport's principal attractions. Justifiably so.

Beneath its original Victorian barrel roof, well over one hundred 'stalls' and small businesses, many of them family-owned, offer an attractive and varied range of goods and produce. From fresh fish, poultry and meats to haberdashery, fashion and jewellery, footwear and baby clothes, gift shops and antiques, there is something to interest everyone! And, of course, there are several cafés offering the market's famous faggots and peas. Delicious! The upstairs gallery also has numerous stalls selling books, records, model kits, stamps, a Bible stall, a souvenir shop, leather goods, memorabilia and quality bric-a-brac. The listing is virtually inexhaustible.

Unlike modern stores, often in the charge of indifferent managers and staff, market shoppers usually deal directly with individual stall-holders.

And the difference is immediately apparent. Here the customer is paramount, and gets a personal, friendly and specialised service whatever their requirements. There is something special to suit all pockets and all tastes.

Some years ago the local council wished to close the old market, demolish it and sell the land to a property developer. They tried their best to persuade the traders to move to the opposite end of the town to the newly opened Kingsway Centre, a modern, all-weather, undercover, two-tier shopping mall. Yet the council had not reckoned on the strength of feeling, not only of the traders themselves, but also the opinions of the townspeople. The traders formed themselves into The Market Tenants Association and were openly defiant to the move. The council were caught unawares and against such fierce opposition to their plan they eventually capitulated, well and truly beaten by 'people power'. A notable victory had been won for small businesses.

Yes, shopping in the market is an unique and pleasurable experience, even though the market is something of an anachronism in an age of out-of-town 'superstores'. Or is it? Innumerable people consider otherwise. For Newport Market is not merely a market - it is an institution, a focal point for shoppers to browse and chart amicably, and for traders to promote their wares. On any day of the week the vibrancy of this bustling market is tangible. Also, the smell of a wide range of fresh produce permeates the air. Wonderful. The loss of such a well-patronised market would leave the town of Newport very much the poorer. May it never happen!

Regency Place

Newport has few buildings of antiquity or of architectural merit; most are typical examples of late Victorian and Edwardian times when the town was a flourishing centre for the worldwide export or coal and iron.

Yet, only a short distance from today's bustling thoroughfare, and about halfway up Stow Hill, is a Regency-style street reminiscent of the Georgian splendour of the spa City of Bath.

Victoria Place was built in 1844 by the firm of Rennie-Logan, builders of the Town Dock alongside the tidal waters of the River Usk. The land for this 'touch of elegance' was generously donated by William Townshend in order 'to provide access to Stow Hill from the South East'. To this very day it does just that.

The street has two facing rows of four-storey 'town houses' which have recently undergone sympathetic modernisation to become a collection of luxury dwellings. The exterior of the terraces are resplendent in their split pastel colours. Each front door with its polished brass is approached by four stone steps. The railings above the basement flats (previously servants' quarters) are painted black; the ornate metalwork on the first-floor balconies are also black with large gold motifs. Even the electric street lamps resemble the original gas lamps.

Without doubt, Victoria Place is an oasis in a desert of architectural mediocrity. So step back in time with a leisurely stroll along its wide pavements... and marvel at its aristocratic appearance. Truly, here stands 'Regency place'.

Stand And Stare

In the centre of Newport stands a remarkable statue to commemorate the life and work of the town's most famous son of modern times, namely, W.H. Davies - the 'Tramp Poet'.

The statue in bronze by Paul Bothwell-Kincaid dominates the lower end of Commercial Street and was commissioned by the Borough Council with assistance from the Welsh Development Agency and the Welsh Arts Council: it was unveiled in 1990 upon the occasion of the 50th anniversary of the poet's death.

Appropriately named 'STAND AND STARE', the theme of this work of art is broadly based around the poet's immortal lines of verse from his short poem 'Leisure':

'What is this life if, full of care,
We have no time to stand and stare.'

Whilst attracting diverse comments as to its cultural merit, the sculpture 'represents a spirit figure enshrined within the body of the tree of life...' and is 'a visually dramatic memorial of man returning to his roots, being evocative of the mysteries of nature, it invites contemplation of the very nature of life...' 'The birds are symbols of thought and imagination that signify the essence of the poet's creativity and freedom of expression'.

William Henry Davies was born on 3rd July, 1871, at the Church House Inn in Portland Street, Pillgwenlly, which was owned by his grand-father, a retired Cornish sea captain. Upon leaving school Davies was apprenticed to a picture-frame maker; the youthful William, though, thirsted for adventure, so much so that at the age of 22 years he journeyed to America where he eventfully lived the life of a tramp, doing any casual work that came his way. His 'hobo' days ended abruptly when he lost his right leg 'jumping trains'; his mobility severely curtailed, he returned to his native land.

Impoverished, he lived in lodging-houses, doing virtually anything to earn enough money to avoid starvation. Significantly, though, his inherent poetic instinct was no longer dormant. He began writing about what moved him the most, the countryside around him and the world of nature. And after 8 years he had saved enough money to publish a slim volume of his poems.

Like all poets, Davies found it far easier to write poems than to get them published. No matter, though, for he persevered and sent a copy of his work to none other than George Bernard Shaw - with a note asking him to either buy it or return it. This proved to be the turning point in his life. For the work of a true, natural genius was instantly recognised. Henceforth, W.H. Davies was able to leave the squalor of his former life and take his place amongst men of integrity and culture.

His subsequent 'Autobiography of a Super - Tramp' brought him to the fore of literary circles and public notice; thereafter, his output of both poetry and prose continued unabated until shortly before his death in 1940.

It is seldom, if ever, that a man's genius should blossom so late in life. For Davies, born and bred in a town, and with but a rudimentary school education, somehow had

an empathy with Mother Nature. His verse is simple, direct and heartfelt - the stuff which endures. This is expressed so eloquently by the following couplet:

'Who sees a cobweb strung with dew pearls, sees
A finer work than jewelled crowns of gold.'

Unlike the average person who simply 'sees', the poet 'perceives' the world around him in a manner bordering on the mystical. This is what sets a poet apart from the rest of society. And W.H. Davies was a true poet, a master of his craft and, arguably, the greatest Nature poet in the English-speaking world.

Incidentally, displayed in Newport Museum is Jacob Epstein's powerful and celebrated bust of Davies himself. A veritable treasure in its own right. And well worth viewing.

A Tale Of An Ox

In the centre of Newport stands an ox. No, not a live ox, but a remarkable sculptured ox fashioned by the highly talented Sebastien Boyeson, the town's resident sculptor between 1993 and 1994. Entitled 'THE VISION OF ST. GWYNLLYW', the work was unveiled for the Borough Council in 1996.

What, then, is the significance of this extraordinary work of art? The life-size replica represents the early siting in the 6th-century of the Cathedral Church of St. Woolos upon the summit of nearby Stow Hill. For according to legend Gwynllyw, a Welsh Chieftain-warrior of Wentloog, was converted to Christianity after experiencing a dream in which he was told to seek out a white ox with a black spot on its forehead and to follow the beast wherever it roamed until it finally came to rest... 'about the banks of the river is a certain mountain where a white ox is seen'. Apparently, this is what he did.

Whether true or not, no matter. And white oxen are but a rare breed. Nonetheless, this remains a highly colourful tale made all the more plausible by its singular lack of reference to the supernatural. Similar 'tales' relate to the siting of churches throughout the Welsh border region.

The history of St. Woolos is well documented: the original mud and wattle structure erected by Gwynllyw and his followers on the hilltop is long gone. And upon this site stands the present-day largely Norman church, a building that indeed can boast a chequered history - a veritable 'Norman jewel in a Gothic casket'.

This austere Cathedral of Wales fought for its religion against overwhelming odds - and has survived! The contemporary poet Glynfab John expresses this eloquently:

St. Woolos

Above the town of Newport kneels
St. Woolos, on Stow Hill:
Her ancient, weather-beaten walls
Confirm faith lives here still.

Cathedral built on firm belief,
She testifies alone
To generations who worshipped
Within her lichened stone.

Unmoved by restless centuries,
She frowns upon a scene
Grey with the grime and guilt of years,
But where faith is ever green.

Resisting change, St. Woolos Church
Proclaims Man's age-old need
To satisfy the hunger-pangs
That bread can never feed.

Surely, a moving and enduring testament to Man's imperishable faith and to the glory of God.

Certainly, the Cathedrals of Wales are no match for the architectural splendour of their English counterparts. But what they lack in visual appeal is more than compensated for by their age. For Cathedrals, such as St. Woolos, St. David's, Llandaff, etc., primitive though they may seem, pre-date the Norman Conquest, long before Christianity had established itself in Britain; they were built at a time when pagan rituals and customs dominated everyday life and superstition was rife.

Finally, the mighty agricultural ox, long regarded by our forefathers as a symbol of fertility, 'designates that this country is to be cultivated'. Who would wish to disagree?

Shadowlands

Much of the coastal plain bordering the Severn Estuary between Newport and Chepstow is designated as a Site of Special Interest due to its abundance of rare flora and fauna.

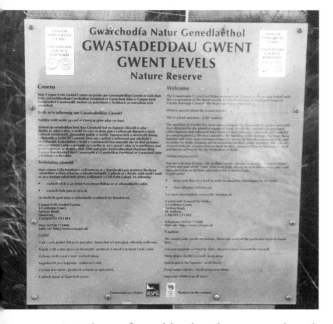

Recently, though, a controversial £10 million artificial wetland reserve has been created on 'The Moors'. An expansive and wind-swept 1,000 acres of grassland stretching from Uskmouth Power Station to Goldcliff was flooded to create a series of salt and freshwater lagoons and reed beds. The reason? To partially compensate for the loss of saline mudflat bird habitats destroyed by the construction of the massive Cardiff Bay Barrage further along the coast.

Opponents of the scheme - environmentalists and aggrieved farmers faced with ruin due to the destruction of their land after generations of good husbandry - argued against the suitability of the Gwent Level to provide proper substitute feeding and breeding-grounds for birds displaced from Cardiff Bay; they maintained that the new reserve would be a 'shadow' of the former

estuarine mudflats of nearby Cardiff which were rich in invertebrate life and a sheltered area for wading birds. One commentator described the new reserve as 'a glorified duckpond' when compared to the 'natural beauty and value of Cardiff Bay'. Hmm... Clearly a contentious issue. To date, however, such concerns appear largely unfounded for there are encouraging signs of over-wintering wildfowl and summer migratory birds descending upon the reserve in huge numbers.

To mark the official opening of the Gwent Levels Wetlands Reserve in March 2000 a commemorative plaque was unveiled by Sir Geoffrey Inkin, chairman of the former Cardiff Bay Development Corporation. Currently, the reserve is managed by the Countryside Council for Wales.

In the coming years this unique and exciting conservation project seems certain to attract very large numbers of nationally important bird species for which it was designed. Birds such as dunlin, teal, redshank and shelduck, widgeon, shoveller, the rarer bittern, bearded tit, amongst others, are all expected to habitate the reserve.

And who knows? Once established, the reserve may well rival the world famous Wildfowl Trust at Slimbridge in Gloucestershire and, likewise, make an equally significant long-term contribution to European wetland wildlife.

Certainly, Gwent Levels Wetlands Reserve offers a wonderful treat for all the family at all times of the year. But remember to wear waterproof footwear and always stick to the site's waymarked paths. An experience not to be missed!

The Shell Grotto

Within the sylvan splendour of Pontypool Park there is much of historical interest and importance. Once at the very heart of a heavily industrialised area of Gwent, one of the town's most curious landmarks is its magnificent Shell Grotto.

Situated high on the brow of the hill overlooking Pontypool, and about a quarter of a mile from the Valley Inheritance Museum, the grotto is believed to have been originally constructed sometime during the 1760s by John Hanbury as a family summer house, a place of peaceful retreat from the everyday cares of industrial life. But it was the equally powerful iron-master Capel Hanbury-Leigh and his wife Molly who together during the 1830s carried out extensive alterations to the grotto, including the spectacular shell decoration.

In 1882 the iron-master played host to his most distinguished guest to the estate, namely, the Prince of Wales (later to become Edward VII); as a member of a shooting party which gathered at the grotto, the Prince will surely have appreciated the fine quality of the workmanship therein. From such a vantage point the views of the surrounding landscape remain to this very day impressive and quite breathtaking.

Inevitably though, with the decline of the industrial era the grotto became much neglected, the object of regular and wanton vandalism: it remained closed to the public for decades. During the winter of 1991 the roof structure partially collapsed. As a public attraction the grotto seemed destined to obscurity.

Yet this highly unusual relic of a bygone age has long had its admirers, those determined to preserve its unique structure and character. And after a lengthy, hardfought campaign, during 1992-93 financial support was forthcoming from CADW, the Welsh Historic Monuments Agency, and the European Regional Development Fund. Work to restore the exterior of the grotto was completed in the summer of 1994.

The campaign to raise additional funds for the laborious and painstaking task of restoring the interior to its former glory continued throughout 1995 - successfully. Finance was again secured from CADW; the grotto then 'hit the jackpot' when it received one of the first Heritage Lottery grants to be awarded in Wales. The restoration of the shell interior begun in 1996 was completed by the end of that year.

The culmination of this endeavour was a grand celebratory re-opening ceremony on 21st May, 1998, amidst considerable media attention. An 1830s-style picnic was staged with actors dressed in period costume portraying local landowner Capel Hanbury-Leigh and his wife Molly.

The grotto itself is unusual in shape, basically circular but not quite, and is built of local sandstone surmounted by an almost conical tiled roof; its plain exterior gives no clue as to what beauty lies within. For the interior design is wholly imaginative. The fanvaulted ceiling springs from six pillars (said originally to have been covered with living ivy), all of which are adorned with thousands of exotic shells interspersed with sharp spar and stars of pure crystal set in geometric and floral patterns. In the centre of the dome large artificial stalactites hang down menacingly. The floor is embedded with various animal bones arranged in various patterns, including a ring of hearts and diamonds. Windows which once held coloured glass gaze outwards upon the surrounding countryside. The original rustic timber chairs have been repaired and returned to their rightful place.

The original interior of shells, crystals and glass was intended to reflect the Romantic period of the time; the design is normally attributed to the Bath architect, S. Gunstan Tit. The decorations were completed in 1844, supposedly by a hermit who made the building his home. Unlikely as this may seem nowadays, in former times it was not altogether unusual for men of substance to install a hermit upon their estates. Such recluses were held in high regard for their powers of perception; throughout their waking hours they pondered matters spiritual and of everyday importance, often reading their musings in prose or verse. Moreover, hermits were a great source of delight - and entertainment - both to their generous benefactors and to their socialite friends.

Fortunately, the Shell Grotto has survived the passage of years and continues to reflect the wealth, extravagance and status of the Hanbury family at that time. It remains one of the finest preserved examples of its kind in the whole of the United Kingdom; this unique folly has become a major tourist attraction in the Torfaen area. And deservedly so! Whilst open only at weekends, the Shell Grotto will surely delight and enthral all who visit it. For its shell-encrusted walls typify the creative and imaginative spirit of man in his unending quest to create works in harmony with nature, works of charm and immense beauty. Brilliant!

The Fountain Of Life

The once common sight of public drinking fountains in villages and towns is long gone. For with the advent of the public water supply such fountains had outlived their usefulness; most fell into disuse and neglect, and gradually disappeared altogether from the everyday scene.

One such fountain that survives still can be found at St. Arvans, near Chepstow, at the entrance to the Wye Valley. The Grade II listed fountain, believed to be one of only two of its kind in the world (a similar one stands in Durban, South Africa), was made from prefabricated parts chosen from the catalogue of Sun Foundry in Glasgow. Two cherubs adorn the upper plinth and the entire structure stands some 9 feet high: it was purchased by public subscription for £25 and declared 'open' on 19th May, 1893.

The fountain was originally located alongside the junction of the Devauden and Tintern roads, but was subsequently moved into the heart of the village in 1934 when the junction was redesigned and the main Chepstow to Monmouth highway widened.

Recently, as part of the village's Millennium celebrations, the fountain was removed for extensive and sympathetic restoration; after many years it is now fully operational again. The cost of the facelift, around £25,000, was funded by CADW, the Welsh Historic Monuments Agency, Monmouthshire County Council, the local community council and the villagers' generous donations. The official re-opening took place on 24th May, 2000.

Today, this fountain stands in its original Victorian livery of dark green. Its waters no longer emanate from an underground spring, but the municipal supply. Nonetheless, the fountain is a reminder of a bygone age when horses bearing heavy loads paused for refreshment at the water trough before continuing upon their weary journey.

A Break With Tradition

Should you fancy a weekend break with a difference (most people do), then visit what is arguably Gwent's most unusual guesthouse - the old lighthouse at St. Brides, Wentloog, on the Gwent Levels.

The West Usk Lighthouse was built in 1821 to help shipping heading for Newport - then a bustling port - to safely navigate the murky and treacherous currents of the River Usk. For hereabouts the Usk ebbs and flows in spectacular fashion, often attaining some 40 feet in height, the greatest rise of any river in Europe. True.

Left unused, empty and virtually derelict (the old lamp room has not been used since 1922), the building suffered much neglect over the years. Then, in 1989, it was purchased by Frank and Danielle Sheahan who set about the formidable task of renovation. Their aim? To offer it to the public as unique Bed & Breakfast accommodation. A year later it opened for business. And what a success story this venture has proved to be.

The old structure has been completely refurbished to a high degree of elegance. Its wedge-shaped rooms are decorated meticulously throughout. A central feature is the original stone spiral staircase; a four-poster bed adorns the master bedroom; and just to add a touch of individuality (or eccentricity) an old red GPO telephone box converted into... a shower! No, do not expect the standard facilities here like televisions and trouser-presses. There are even plans to turn on the powerful lamp again. But not to shine outwards into the estuary, rather to attract travellers to this haven of peace and tranquillity.

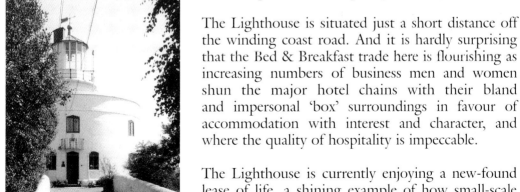

The Lighthouse is situated just a short distance off the winding coast road. And it is hardly surprising that the Bed & Breakfast trade here is flourishing as increasing numbers of business men and women shun the major hotel chains with their bland and impersonal 'box' surroundings in favour of accommodation with interest and character, and where the quality of hospitality is impeccable.

The Lighthouse is currently enjoying a new-found lease of life, a shining example of how small-scale private enterprise can be a winner. Yes, the future is bright!

A Different Perspective

Every year tens of thousands of tourists flock to the Wye Valley to marvel at its scenic beauty and much-vaunted attractions. Understandably so. Nowhere is this more apparent than at Tintern. For beside the graceful sweep of the River Wye stands Tintern Abbey, majestic in ruin, a miracle in stone and a fitting testimony to man's imperishable faith in the Almighty.

However, centuries ago Tintern was far from the rural idyll it appears to be today. No. Here stood a prosperous industrial centre with smelting furnaces and forges incessantly belching smoke and grime to darken the sunlit sky, and mighty hammers rhythmically beating iron bars into fine strands of wire; also, where poverty and deprivation were rife.

During Elizabethan times, in 1566, a wireworks was established at Tintern in the lower Angidy Valley, just a few minutes stroll from the Abbey. This was founded in response to the unwelcome import of wire from abroad; oddly, though, German 'know-how' and labour were brought to the area! Herein lies Tintern's chief claim to industrial fame - the very first wireworks in Britain to harness 'water-power' rather than 'man-power' in the wire-drawing process. Perfectly true.

Such was the success of the operation that in 1606 a similar wireworks was established a few miles away at Whitebrook to cope with the ever-growing demand that Tintern alone could not meet.

In the late 17th-century a blast furnace and three forges were active at Tintern: by the middle of the 18th-century the complex of iron and wireworks had spread along a 2-mile stretch of the Angidy Valley and into the Fedw. A forge was operational at Pont-y-Saeson in 1675. The raw materials necessary to produce and work the iron, namely, iron ore, limestone, wood (for charcoal), and later coal, were all readily available locally.

A series of reservoirs and leats had been constructed upon the Angidy River to provide

a plentiful supply of fast-flowing water to power machinery. Incredibly, by 1821 there were no fewer than eighteen huge waterwheels driving the immense bellows and hammers of the works and mills between the upper reaches and the Wye far below.

Wire, nails and tin plate manufactured at Tintern were shipped from Tintern Dock and Wharf to the burgeoning ports of Bristol, Cardiff and Swansea. But with the opening of the Wye Valley Railway during 1876, the bulk of output was transferred to the faster railway network.

Industry flourished at Tintern until the end of the 19th-century. Nowadays there is little evidence of its former glory apart from the ruins of the lower Angidy ironworks which were excavated in the early 1980s and made safe; the site is open to the public. The reservoirs or 'fish ponds' survive and are admired as natural features, their fresh waters well-stocked with trout; the waterwheels are long gone except one which has been restored to full working order and can be seen at the former sawmill adjoining the main road.

Yes, Tintern has much to be proud of. Times change and society 'moves on'. Man's inventive ability and insatiable desire for development, though, remains ever constant. The lower Angidy Valley bears silent witness to this. A visit to this picturesque backwater amply rewards the more enlightened tourist.

The Cherry Tree

Imagine a pub with only one ale on tap. Difficult? Of course. Yet unlikely as it may seem the tiny Cherry Tree Inn at Tintern is just such a pub. Nestling in the rural splendour of the Angidy Valley and slightly off the Devauden road, this alehouse has been quenching the thirst of loyal regulars for some 300 years.

The pub serves neither lager nor stout; draught bitter (Hancock's HB) and Bulmer's traditional draught cider are on offer, each cool glass dispensed directly from the cask in the back room. Delicious! Unlike hostelries elsewhere the Cherry Tree is no modern 'mega' pub. It has few available facilities; no bar snacks, no 'canned' background music, no television, no juke box, no one-armed bandit and no pool table.

What, then, is the appeal of this one-room bar? The answer should be obvious. Within its ancient rough-stone walls awaits a friendly welcome rarely found in more prestigious plasticy and sterile 'watering-holes'. In such quaint and old-fashioned surroundings the stresses of everyday life are easily banished and replaced by the almost forgotten art of convivial conversation. Even the games here are all totally low-tech. Traditional games like darts, cribbage and Victorian bar skittles (the green baize table game involving little wooden mushrooms) remain as popular as ever with the 'regulars'.

With good cause the Cherry Tree has been much appreciated by countless generations; in 1892 it even figured as part of a wedding present to the Duke of Beaufort. Furthermore, it is one of only two pubs in the whole of Wales to have featured annually for over two decades in the Campaign for Real Ale's (CAMRA) 'GOOD BEER GUIDE'. Quite an achievement!

Surprisingly, the Welsh monuments group CADW has no policy for preserving historic pubs (unlike its English counterpart, English Heritage). Thus, the long-term future of the Cherry Tree cannot necessarily be guaranteed.

Owned and ably served by Doug and Doris Knight for well over 40 years, all attempts to modernise the pub were fiercely resisted - much to the relief of its patrons. Their son, Alan, the current landlord, recently put the pub up for sale. With no sale forthcoming after several months, he reconsidered the position.

This single-bar gem has remained largely unspoilt by the passage of time and is a shrine for pub purists whose notion of the perfect pub is somewhere to relax around a crackling log fire and chat amicably with friends and acquaintances - whilst, of course, having a pint of the finest cask ale or draught cider at hand.

The Cherry Tree Inn is an unique pub. And it is to be hoped that this venerable drinking establishment will continue to satisfy the needs of the local community for many years to come. Hear! Hear!

King Of Terrors

In the early 19th-century, Tredegar and the surrounding area were very much in the vanguard of industrial expansion. The renowned iron-master, Samuel Homfray, had begun operations at Tredegar ironworks in 1801: the rapidly expanding township grew around these ironworks.

Overcrowding in the workers' homes was common and sanitation non-existent; the only drinking water was heavily contaminated. Against such a background of appalling squalor it was, perhaps, inevitable that outbreaks of cholera should strike the beleaguered community, firstly in 1831 and then again in 1849.

Details of the first epidemic are scanty; more is recorded of the 1849 outbreak. The first victim was an Inland Revenue Officer named T. Price, who resided in a more prosperous area of the town at Charles Street. By midday two healthy men in the same street had succumbed to the disease. Within less than a month there was scarcely a street in the town unaffected by the 'King of Terrors'.

So contagious was the disease that an entire family residing in Charles Street was wiped out within a day. The mother died in the morning, her two children during the afternoon; the father helped an aged midwife place the corpses of his beloved ones in coffins 'as they were brought by the undertaker'. Sadly, by ten o'clock that evening the poor man himself was a corpse. And before daybreak the midwife, too, had fallen victim to the dreaded disease and 'was no more'.

As the death toll rose alarmingly, and with doctors unable to control the epidemic, large numbers of terror-stricken inhabitants abandoned their homes and (as in the outbreak of 1831) fled to the countryside to escape the scourge.

But where could the dead be buried? Fearing contamination to consecrated burial grounds, and contrary to Christian teaching, bigoted clerics issued a circular declaring the town's graveyards 'closed against those who died from cholera'. Unbelievable! And so a separate cholera cemetery was established at Cefn Golau ('The Hill of Light') on the outskirts of the town.

When a funeral cortege journeyed through the streets of Tredegar towards the cemetery, doors were closed and bolted, passers-by hurried out of sight, and undertakers often struggled to find enough bearers to convey the hapless victims to their final resting place. Camphor and all sorts of 'preventatives were worn by the majority of people day and night as an attempt at a prophylactic'.

Belatedly, the authorities (and the iron-masters) were roused into action. Hitherto, public health was a matter of little concern. But with a worsening situation and under such public pressure, drastic action became the order of the day. Ditches and drains were emptied and copiously sprayed with disinfectant, piles of rotting household rubbish removed from the streets, backyard piggeries outlawed, and laws for preserving general health stringently enforced.

In times of great sorrow and anguish many bereaved people turn in desperation to religious faith for solace. Following the horrific outbreaks of 1831 and 1849 the chapels and churches in Tredegar were regularly packed. Yet as each epidemic abated, places of worship became less frequented as previously terrified converts 'went their own way'.

Today, the eerie and isolated cemetery at Cefn Golau is a forlorn place. Headstones inscribed in Welsh stand aslant, weathered gray by the passage of years. They tell a sad story of families ravaged by the disease and provide a stark reminder of early industrial life when the basic facilities of sanitation and hygiene were unavailable to the local community. Thankfully, in this respect, times have changed for the better!

Stonewalled

For centuries, hill-farmers have chosen to mark the borders of their land with dry-stone walls. Such walls were laboriously built by hand from stone found locally; no bonding agent such as cement was available in days gone by - nor needed. The sheer weight of the interlocking flat stones was sufficient to hold the wall together.

The fact that the majority of dry-stone walls have endured the weathering of the ages is in itself quite remarkable. For modern composites, such as mortar and cement, whilst purporting to possess superior properties, have already proven to be susceptible to the vagaries of the elements.

Visitors to the Crown Business Park at Tredegar will therefore be more than a little surprised to meet a sweeping 140-yard dry-stone wall. The purpose for its construction, organised by Blaenau Gwent County Borough Council with aid from the Welsh Development Agency, was to contribute towards an attractive working environment for 21st-century business and commerce; also to create a distinctively Welsh country setting in an industry-scarred area; and to echo the geology and harmonise with the surrounding landscape.

The wall, certainly pleasing to the eye, was built in 1999 by Paul Horne and Brandon Warlow with the assistance of Alan Jones, three of Wales' foremost dry-stone wallers, or 'dykers'.

Will this new dry-stone wall, an anachronism by any standard, stand the test of time? Certainly. For the durability of natural material such as stone is assured. Strange to think that this 'modern' wall is very much an example of 'back to the future'!

A-Spire To Heaven

Anyone approaching the hilltop village of Trellech on the Chepstow to Monmouth ridge-road must surely be amazed by the impressive, soaring spire of the village church, a fine and proud building dominating the skyline for miles around.

Trellech was once a considerably larger, thriving village than it is nowadays. Established in the Middle Ages by the de Clares, Norman Marcher Lords, it became one of the wealthiest market towns in South Wales, enjoying Borough status with its own charter and town seal. It even had its own Magistrates' Court which functioned until as recently as 1974.

What, then, sent Trellech into an irreversible decline? Due to some silly dispute over the poaching of deer, the town was ransacked by Lord Bigod of Chepstow in 1291. Houses were torched and the townspeople callously slain. Yet the town recovered to prosper again. But further afflictions were to follow. As elsewhere, the Black Death had a devastating effect upon the community. And in 1404 that fiery champion of the Welsh cause, Owain Glyndŵr, and his rampaging troops wreaked havoc in the 'English' town. Thereafter, the township steadily became depopulated; by 1700 Trellech was described as being 'now reduced to a poore inconsiderable village' - the small and picturesque village it is today.

The mighty church of St. Nicholas dates from the late 13th-century and is built on the site of a much earlier structure. Within its hallowed walls are many antiquities. Most prominent of these is a massive, gabled, stone sundial dated 1689; this was presented to the village by Lady Magdalen Probert, the widow of Sir George Probert of Pantglas. What is unusual is that its pedestal is decorated on three sides in relief with crude carvings showing the outstanding 'wonders' of Trellech - in short, an early guide book in stone!

The front face displays the three Neolithic or Bronze Age standing stones, popularly known as Harold's Stones, situated on the outskirts of the village. Over them is inscribed MAJOR SAXIS, and under, HIC FUIT VICTOR HARALDUS.

An adjacent face depicts the Virtuous Well, a chalybeate well set in meadowland to the south-east of the village. For centuries a place famous for the healing powers of its iron-laden waters, of pilgrimage and divine worship, the figure of the well is accompanied by MAXIMA FONTE and DOM MAGD PROBERT OSTENDIT.

A third face shows the Terret Tump, an artificial tumulus some 40 feet high with a large surrounding moat, at the rear of Court Farm close to the church, and most probably the earthworks of an early Norman motte and bailey castle. Above the tumulus is inscribed MAGNA MOLE, and beneath, O QUOT HIC SEPULTI.

The faces of the sundial itself are incised with the hours of the day. On the upper part appears HORA DIEM DE PASCIT EUNDO - 'The hour passing devours the day'. How very apt.

Other relics worthy of inspection include an Elizabethan chalice, the church plate dated 1576 and a pewter flagon of 1620 inscribed with rows of undecipherable numerals; a brightly coloured coat-of-arms of Charles II dated 16 CR 83 and given in recognition of the support the village gave the Royalist cause; also, a round stone font reputedly of Saxon origin.

The panelled oak pulpit dated 1640 with its floral carving was once part of a 'three-decker' pulpit and the oak sanctuary rails are formed of 'barley-sugar' twists. The thick Elizabethan studded oak door in the south porch bears on the inside the date 1595 together with the sacred monogram, both of inlaid lead.

The Early English interior is graced by fine arcades and lofty arches. Most of the memorial stones belong to the Rumsey family who lived at Trellech Court from the 16th-century until the middle of the 19th-century.

Outside in the churchyard stands an 8th-century Celtic preaching cross. Beside it is a strange stone altar some 8 feet long, 3 feet wide, and an incredible 1 foot thick resting on stone blocks incised with much-worn Celtic carvings of crosses in circles. The purpose of this 'Druid's Altar' is uncertain. Perhaps it was indeed originally intended for pagan ritual sacrifice.

The peaceful and sleepy village that is Trellech today belies its historic past. For Trellech Church with its slender spire rising heavenwards surely expresses a spirit of restrained exaltation, a veritable prayer in stone. Here, indeed, is a splendid place in which to while away an hour or two in quietude and idle contemplation. Wonderful!

The Malt Barn

Discover Gwent Rural Life Museum in the charming old market town of Usk. Housed in an ancient stone Malt Barn and other buildings in New Market Street, the museum portrays all aspects of life in the Welsh border country from Victorian times until the end of the Second World War; from domestic life to the agricultural and from hand tool crafts to mechanisation, they are all represented.

The museum is highly unusual in being wholly independent of local authority control: it is run entirely by volunteers. Its exhibits, which number many thousands, have all been donated by the generosity of local people over the past 30 years or more. In 1983 the museum won recognition with a Prince of Wales Award for its excellence. And deservedly so.

Adjoining the Malt Barn is a Victorian kitchen filled with the utensils and gadgets of a bygone age plus a laundry, all of which are certain to bring a smile to the face of today's housewife. Another wing houses a cobbler's shop and saddlery, together with displays of pig-keeping and thatching; the nearby dairy contains milking machinery and a comprehensive collection of butter and cheese-making equipment. The visitor leaves the main building through a sturdy timber cell door from Usk's old House of Correction.

Outside, the yard at the rear of the building contains the impressive blacksmith's shop. Two new barns, one opened in 1989 and the other in 1995, contain fascinating displays of carpentry, cider-making and coopering, milling equipment, woodland crafts, farming implements, and transport by horse and engine. Enthusiasts

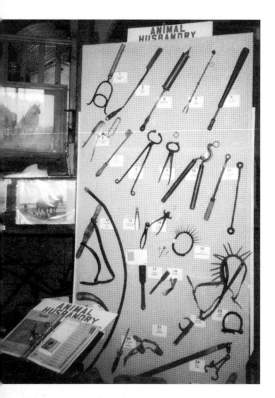

of vintage agricultural machinery will delight in the well-preserved exhibits that were formerly used during the seasons of the year.

Incidentally, the museum is only a few yards away from the 18th-century stone bridge which gracefully arches its way across the sparkling waters of the Usk, a river renowned for its salmon fishing. A leisurely stroll along its gently sloping banks is without rival at any time of the year and amply rewards those attuned to a rural environment. Annually, throughout the summer months, the town itself is profusely decked with colourful blooms; in recent years Usk has won the Wales in Bloom competition on several occasions.

Without doubt, the Rural Life Museum is a veritable treasure for young and old alike. For some it provides a nostalgic experience where cherished memories of a not-too-distant past are recalled. By contrast, there is plenty to intrigue and enthral younger visitors; they can gain an insight into Victorian and early 20th-century children at work.

Adults who visit the museum will surely reflect upon the extent to which life within the home nowadays has become easier with the multiplicity of 'labour-saving' appliances. Yet, are the products of modern technology as reliable as the simpler, tried and tested, old-fashioned methods and machines? Hmm....

Where The Devil Broke His Apron-Strings

An unusual title, yes. But an appropriate one, nonetheless. Over centuries, folk born and brought up in the lower Sirhowy Valley felt such a place was surrounded with an aura of mystery, terror even - and best avoided.

For the awesome place where 'The Devil Broke His Apron-Strings' is little more than a very long and jagged scar, a deep chasm which to this day disfigures the brackened brow of Mynydd Machen. Its position high on the steeply wooded slopes of the mountain extends from the lower end of Wattsville to the outskirts of Cross Keys. As to its depth, it is seemingly bottomless; a pebble dropped into it gives no sound of striking bottom. Very scary.

The huge rent is a permanent reminder of an ages-past upheaval of the earth's continually changing outer crust. Our forefathers, in their ignorance and unquestioning belief, knew nothing of Geology, strata, faults, etc. Thus, to the elderly folk in their Hell-centred innocence a simple geological fault, a landslip, became invested with poetic imagery.

In the former colliery village of Wattsville youngsters were warned repeatedly from an early age to stay well away from the place, the entrance to the underworld; for the Devil himself was lurking unseen to prey upon little children who ventured too close and triumphantly take them down to eternal damnation in the fires of Hades, never to return home again to their families and friends. And in the still darkness of a hot summer's night, when the Devil left his underground crypt to roam the valley unbridled and cast his satanic spell, the sulphurous, choking smell of brimstone tainted the fragrant air. Such a story would surely hold any small child spellbound and strike fear into an impressionable young mind.

During the days of the Temperance League and the Band of Hope which forbade the consumption of any form of intoxicating liquor, the scar's very existence was an incisive and visible reminder to sinners and those who veered off the 'straight and narrow' that retribution was only 'a stone's throw' away on the opposite side of the valley. The adults knew exactly what this meant.

'Where The Devil Broke His Apron-Strings' remains an enigma, but it is there for all to see. The fault is hard to locate from the other side of the valley; its huge, gaping mouth deceptively overgrown with leafy green trees and colourful displays of purple heather, bluebells, foxgloves, bracken and the delicious small blue fruit of hardy whimberry bushes. Yet even on the hottest day in summer this place stays chillingly cold and an eerie silence pervades the air.

Directly below the jagged scar was once the thriving pre-Industrial Revolution community of Full Moon. Sadly, its death-knell was the incursion of the steam railway which literally tore the prosperous community into two halves; many cottages in the iron-rail's path were unceremoniously demolished - in the name of progress. Some progress, as subsequent events of 100 years later were to prove with the closure and removal of the line.

To this very day the older people of the lower Sirhowy Valley, brought up on a diet of superstition, ritual and folklore, regard 'Where The Devil Broke His Apron-Strings' as a real place, magical yet eloquently terrifying. Curiously enough, the place

actually appears on the Geological Survey Map of 1902 named as 'The Devil's Apronful'. Perhaps the older generations had access to knowledge no longer available to present-day, technologically-orientated society. Time alone may well tell.

And despite the arrival of the new millennium and a new age of enlightenment - the age of Aquarius - people of all religious persuasions still cling to the time-held beliefs in the Devil and Hell - just in case.

Conclusion

Yes, I have thoroughly enjoyed writing this sequel to *'Glimpses Of Gwent'*. I earnestly hope this volume will prove equally appealing. And, finally, let me be permitted to express my innermost feelings about the magical and mystical land of Gwent as perceived by the poet Glynfab John.

Praise To The One

Praise to The One who fashioned Gwent,
and conjured up this magic place.
Let others dwell in shires like Kent,
and live with dignity and grace.

Mine is a land of hidden byways,
the Severn Sea and mountains steep.
Eternity seems but mere days
while such as Tintern Abbey sleep.

Give me the secret haunts of Wentwood,
the mystery of hills and vales.
Strange omens stir my Celtic blood,
enchanted by the myths of Wales.

Praise to The One who created Gwent,
the truly Supreme Artist ... God.
And finally, all yearning spent,
Let me remain where Saints once trod.

What else is there to say? Iechyd Da!!!

Acknowledgements

I wish to express my sincere thanks to those individuals and organisations who have assisted me in the preparation of this book.

In particular, I am greatly indebted to my father, Glynfab John, for permission to include his poems **'St Woolos'** and **'Praise To The One'**; also, for his meticulous correction, where necessary, of the text.

Likewise, to my close friend Mary Meredith for her commendable patience when typing the entire manuscript.

In addition, I am grateful to the following for permission to photograph relevant exhibits: The Nelson Museum & Local History Centre, Monmouth; Ron Inglis, Museum & Heritage Officer, Newport Museum and Tredegar House; the Trustees and Staff of Usk Rural Life Museum; CADW, the Welsh Historic Monuments Agency (likewise for cover illustration).

Photographs for *'Shadowlands'* were kindly supplied by Adam Rowlands, Warden, Gwent Levels Wetlands Reserve.

The drawing by Winsor Grimes of the ornamental gates at 'Three Springs', Monkswood, is hereby acknowledged, though I have been unsuccessful in tracing the artist.

Photographs not credited above are drawn from the Author's personal collection amassed over recent years.

Finally, I pay tribute to those authors who down the centuries have been motivated to extol the virtues of 'a green and smiling land' that is the unique border County of Gwent.

G.D.J.
September 2001